Whether you are exploring new challenges or a lifestyle change, striving for a broader client base or refocusing your career path, Conduit can provide you with the resources and personalized attention to meet your professional goals. Our mission is to find a match that best meets your professional objectives.

WITHDRAWN

conduit

Connecting people to jobs.

MSU/Detroit College of Law

full service legal search   www.conduitrecruiting.com

The media's watching Vault!
Here's a sampling of our coverage.

"Lawyers looking for the scoop on the nation's biggest law firms now have a place to go."
– *The Wall Street Journal*

"With reviews and profiles of firms that one associate calls 'spot on', [Vault's] guide has become a key reference for those who want to know what it takes to get hired by a law firm and what to expect once they get there."
– *New York Law Journal*

"The best place on the web to prepare for a job search."
– *Fortune*

"Vault is indispensable for locating insider information."
– *Metropolitan Corporate Counsel*

"[Vault's guide] is an INVALUABLE Cliff's Notes to prepare for interviews."
– *Women's Lawyer's Journal*

"For those hoping to climb the ladder of success, [Vault's] insights are priceless."
– *Money Magazine*

"[Vault guides] make for excellent starting points for job hunters and should be purchased by academic libraries for their career sections [and] university career centers."
– *Library Journal*

> the most trusted name in career information™

VAULT GUIDE TO LITIGATION LAW CAREERS

VAULT GUIDE TO LITIGATION LAW CAREERS

NEERAJA VISWANATHAN, JD AND
THE STAFF OF VAULT

ACKNOWLEDGMENTS

Matt Doull, Ahmad Al-Khaled, Lee Black, Eric Ober, Hollinger Ventures, Tekbanc, New York City Investment Fund, Globix, Hoover's, Glenn Fischer, Mark Hernandez, Ravi Mhatre, Carter Weiss, Ken Cron, Ed Somekh, Isidore Mayrock, Zahi Khouri, Sana Sabbagh, and other Vault investors, as well as our family and friends.

Neeraja's acknowledgements:

I am grateful to all the attorneys and school officials who agreed to speak with me regarding this book. Thanks to Marcy Lerner and Vera Djordjevich for their careful editing and advice. I would also like to thank my friends and family, both in SF and NYC, who kept me company during the long hours spent writing this book. Special thanks to Gil Allison, who taught me the value of networking.

Why Weil?

Best Law Firm of the Americas

– Global Counsel (2002)

**On the "most wanted"
list of general counsels**

– Corporate Board Member

**Tied for 1st place among
all U.S. law firms in
intellectual property litigation**

– IP Worldwide (2002)

AUSTIN
BOSTON
BRUSSELS
BUDAPEST
DALLAS
FRANKFURT
HOUSTON
LONDON
MIAMI
NEW YORK
PARIS
PRAGUE
SILICON VALLEY
SINGAPORE
WARSAW
WASHINGTON, DC

www.weil.com

 WEIL, GOTSHAL & MANGES LLP

Table of Contents

INTRODUCTION   1

THE SCOOP   3

Chapter 2: Litigation Basics   5

What is Litigation? 5
Lawsuits and Trials 6
The Court System 7
Sources of Law 9

Chapter 3: Types of Litigation Practice   13

Civil Litigation 13
Criminal Litigation 20
Appellate Practice 23
Public Interest Litigation 24

GETTING HIRED   27

Chapter 4: The Law School Experience   29

The First Step: Getting In 30
The First Year: Be Prepared 36
The Second and Third Years 42
Beyond the Classroom 44

Chapter 5: Job Search Basics   49

The Hiring Process 49
The Resume 52
Mastering the Interview 56

Chapter 6: The Second Summer Internship   63

Big Law 63
Government Positions 69
Judicial Clerkships 70

Sailors know.

It's called teaming.

We're a law firm with an uncommon practice—organizing our practice around clients. Not your typical service team of complex litigators or workout lawyers, but a crew of professionals from diverse practice areas. All focused around the client's business, issues and opportunities. All on the same course.

To learn more about doing high performance work as part of a high performing team, visit us at www.pillsburywinthrop.com

Teams that work.

PILLSBURY WINTHROP LLP

www.pillsburywinthrop.com

Chapter 7: The Bar Exam and Beyond   75

Overview of the Bar Exam 75

Chapter 8: Leading Employers and Recruiters   81

Top Ranked Litigation Firms 82

Legal Recruiter Directory 87

ON THE JOB   91

Chapter 9: A Litigator's Skills   93

Legal Writing: The Pen is Mightier 93

Legal Research: The Library and the Computer 95

Communication Skills: If it Please the Court .96

Organization: First Things First 97

It's Who You Are... 100

Frustrations 101

Chapter 10: Litigation Career Paths   105

Civil Litigations 105

Criminal Litigation 117

Other Public and Private Service Litigators .126

Chapter 11: The Role of the Junior Litigator   131

Legal Documents 131

Success On the Job 137

Changing Jobs 139

Final Analysis 140

APPENDIX   143

Sample Legal Forms 145

Glossary of Terms 159

About the Author 167

Psst...
Need a Change in Venue?

Use the Internet's most targeted

job search tools for law

professionals.

Vault Law Job Board

The most comprehensive and convenient job board for law professionals. Target your search by area of law, function, and experience level, and find the job openings that you want. No surfing required.

VaultMatch Resume Database

Vault takes match-making to the next level: post your resume and customize your search by area of law, experience and more. We'll match job listings with your interests and criteria and e-mail them directly to your inbox.

VAULT
> the most trusted name in career information™

Introduction

If you have dreams of becoming a lawyer and your mind is filled with images of trials, witnesses and every courtroom drama you've ever seen on television, then you're thinking of becoming a litigator.

There are basically two types of lawyers: litigators and transactional attorneys. Transactional attorneys are rarely, if ever, in court. Instead, they make deals, draft agreements and handle transactions – the merging of two companies, the incorporation of a business, establishing a trust for a client's children. The work of litigation attorneys, on the other hand, almost always revolves around the courtroom. Not all litigators are trial lawyers, but most have to plan for trial and draft the necessary paperwork of pleadings, pre-trial motions and legal briefs. Even if they never get into court – and many litigators do not – their job centers on the possibility of court and a trial.

Litigation can be an exciting career. It certainly is a demanding one. America is the most litigious country in the world, with hundreds of lawsuits filed every few minutes. The American court system is complicated and very few people enter into a lawsuit without a lawyer by their side. The litigator's job is to navigate the legal system and interpret the relevant laws, to ensure the fair treatment of, and try to obtain the best result for, her client. Litigators shoulder enormous responsibility; at stake may be a large sum of money, a client's livelihood or freedom, and possibly even his life.

Litigation is seldom as dramatic as the cases you see on television, and there is no one kind of person who becomes a litigator. The media likes to focus on moments of drama, but litigation offers a steady career with a wide variety of opportunities for the eager law student. If you're curious to know whether you have what it takes to become a litigator and what your life would be like, keep reading.

THE SCOOP

Chapter 2: Litigation Basics

Chapter 3: Types of Litigation Practice

Litigation Basics

What is Litigation?

Litigation is always in the news – from the controversial landmark abortion case, Roe v. Wade, to the O.J. Simpson trials to the environmental class action lawsuits portrayed in the films *Erin Brockovich* and *A Civil Action*. A litigation is a legal proceeding between two or more parties. A litigator is a lawyer who represents a party in litigation. Because litigation is an adversarial proceeding between opposing parties, most of a litigator's job involves preparing for trial, even if a negotiated settlement is the ultimate goal.

In cases where parties have contracted to resolve their disputes out of court, a mediator can be hired to find an amicable compromise between the parties. This mediation (or, in some cases, arbitration) reduces the number of cases that go to trial so the already crowded courts are not completely overwhelmed.

Criminal proceedings

There are two kinds of litigation: civil and criminal. When someone breaks a state or federal law, he commits an offense against society. The government, on behalf of the community, begins a criminal proceeding to hold the offender responsible. A criminal litigation is therefore between the government and the accused, or defendant. The government is represented by a prosecutor, typically a district attorney (for state prosecutions) or a federal prosecutor (for federal crimes). The defendant is represented by either a private criminal attorney or a public defender appointed by the state. (Occasionally, usually against the advice of both his lawyer and the judge, a defendant chooses to represent himself, or acts pro se.)

Most states divide crimes into misdemeanors and felonies. A misdemeanor is any offense that results in less than one year of jail time. Petty theft, possession of a small amount of drugs, or breaking and entering is some examples of misdemeanors. Many misdemeanors can result in a fine or instead of jail time. Felonies are more serious offenses that virtually always result in prison terms of more than one year and may include a fine as well as incarceration. Murder, racketeering, rape and kidnapping are all felony offenses. In some states, serious felonies, such as the murder of a policeman or murder with premeditation, are capital offenses, in which cases a criminal defendant might face the death penalty. A person accused of a crime is presumed innocent until proven guilty beyond a reasonable doubt.

Civil actions

A civil action encompasses virtually any non-criminal court proceeding. It can be a private action between two citizens, a proceeding by one person against the state, a suit by an individual against a corporation or any combination thereof. The party bringing the suit, known as the plaintiff or petitioner, usually is seeking a sum of money (damages) from another party (the defendant or respondent) to compensate her for a claimed injury or loss. Sometimes the remedy sought involves not money but performance; one party wants the court to compel another either to do something he is obligated to do or to stop doing something that is injurious to one bringing suit. In a civil action, the case turns not on the defendant's guilt but on the issue of liability – a party is found either liable or not liable. The burden of proof required to establish liability in a civil suit is generally a lower threshold than the "guilt beyond a reasonable doubt" required in a criminal trial.

In the case of both criminal and civil litigation, the parties may never actually make it to court; they might come to a mutual compromise before the trial date. Parties to a civil suit might reach a financial agreement or other settlement, while the prosecution and defense in a criminal case might agree to a plea bargain, under which a prosecutor offers a reduced charge or sentence in exchange for the defendant's plea of guilt.

Lawsuits and Trials

A lawsuit is filed at the trial level. A trial might be in front of a jury or just a judge (known as a bench trial). In criminal actions, a defendant has the right to a speedy trial. There is no such right for parties in civil cases, and many civil actions go on for years. Most litigation will never even reach a courtroom – the parties might settle, one side might withdraw from the suit or a judge might dismiss the case before trial.

A trial entails everything you see on television: a judge, a jury, a variety of evidence, opposing lawyers and two parties. During the trial, the jury considers questions of fact: Did Mr. Hughes kill his wife? Was the car crash an accident? Was XYZ Company negligent in manufacturing faulty women's lingerie? Did the wire in the plaintiff's bra actually cause the injury she claims it did? The jury is there to decide these questions, using only the evidence presented in court. Before and during the course of the trial, there are also questions of law to be addressed by the judge: Should photos of Mr. Hughes' bedroom be allowed into evidence? Is the testimony of XYZ's chief designer admissible? Should the fact that juror number three slept through the testimony result in a mistrial?

The judge decides questions of law, usually after both parties have presented their arguments. In making her decision, the judge relies on previous case law and the relevant rules of civil and criminal procedure. (You can see questions of law being decided on *Law & Order* and *The Practice* when the lawyers meet the judge in chambers before trial, usually to request that she exclude a piece of the prosecutor's evidence for one reason or another. In real life, before making such a decision the judge would review lengthy written memoranda from all lawyers involved).

When the trial is over, the losing party often has the opportunity to appeal the decision to an appellate court. The role of the appeals court is not to second-guess the jury's or judge's rulings on the facts; at the appellate level, only questions of law can be reviewed. The appellate court hears from both sides to decide, essentially, if the trial was conducted properly. If the appeals court concludes that a question of law was not properly decided by the trial judge, it can reverse or overturn the lower court's decision – essentially negating it – or it can remand the case, asking the lower court to reconsider the case in light of the appellate court's opinion. A reversal is often followed by a remand. In the case of Mr. Hughes' murder trial, an appellate court would not decide whether or not Mr. Hughes killed his wife – the jury already concluded that he did – but it can find that the photos of his bedrrom were improperly admitted into evidence. The court might then overturn the guilty verdict and remand the case back to the lower court for a new trial in which the jury will not be able to consider those photographs as evidence.

An appellate court is rarely seen on television, but the decisions of appeals courts are very important, not only to the parties involved but to future litigants in the same jurisdiction.

The Court System

State and federal courts each have jurisdiction, or legal authority, over certain matters. Jurisdiction is conferred upon the courts, ultimately, from the United States Constitution. Jurisdiction can be geographical (that is, within the borders of a state) or because of the subject matter (antitrust litigation, for example, is a federal matter). Without jurisdiction, a court has no authority over a case or its parties.

Both the federal and state court systems are structured like pyramids; each level has greater authority and jurisdiction over a wider geographic region than the level below. At the bottom are the local trial courts, the courts of first instance. Above the trial courts sit the intermediate courts of appeal, which hear appeals from the trial-level courts. At the very top is the highest appellate court, which usually agrees to hear only select appeals from the intermediate courts of appeal.

The federal court system

The highest court in the country, in both the federal and state systems, is the Supreme Court of the United States in Washington, D.C. Nine justices, appointed by the president with the advice and consent of the Senate, sit on the Supreme Court bench. The Supreme Court accepts only a small number of cases to review each term, and its decisions are binding on courts at both a state and federal level. Below the Supreme Court are the federal appeals courts. There are 13 circuit courts of appeal, 12 of which are regional and one of which, the U.S. Court of Appeals for the Federal Circuit, hears only cases concerning certain subject matter. Each circuit has a Supreme Court justice assigned as a circuit justice as well as a panel of circuit court judges appointed by the president.

The circuit courts hear appeals from the federal trial courts of general jurisdiction, the 94 district courts of the United States and Puerto Rico. The federal court system also includes courts of special jurisdiction that hear only cases concerning specific subject matter. For example, each federal district has a bankruptcy court to hear petitions from those seeking relief under the U.S. Bankruptcy Code. Other specialized courts include the U.S. Tax Court, the U.S. Court of Federal Claims and the U.S. Court of International Trade.

Federal court jurisdiction encompasses cases involving federal laws, the federal constitution, the United States government, controversies between states or between the United States and foreign governments, disputes arising at sea, and controversies between residents of two different states that involve more than $75,000.

State court systems

Each state has its own court system, paralleling the federal structure. At the lowest level are the general trial courts, whose names differ from state to state. In Iowa, for example, the trial courts are called district courts, while in California they are superior courts. Up one level is an intermediate appellate court, which hears appeals from the trial courts. Then, at the top of the system, with statewide jurisdiction, is the highest court of appeal of the state, frequently known as the state's supreme court. (Somewhat confusingly, New York's trial courts are called supreme courts while the highest court in New York is the Court of Appeals).

Most legal disputes go to state courts rather than to federal courts. State courts also have sole jurisdiction over certain cases, such as probate matters, real estate questions, juvenile issues, most criminal cases and contract disputes. Like the federal system, state court systems have certain specialized courts that handle only particular subject matters. States have family courts for divorces, adoption and child custody hearings. They may also have probate courts to handle estate matters and special courts to hear tax disputes or claims against the state government.

Sources of Law

Precedent

You will often hear litigators talking about research into case law or the case they are working on. A case is a general term for any dispute brought before a court. So when a litigator is talking about his "case," he means the litigation suit that he is currently working on. The word "case," however, has a double meaning – it also refers to a court's written decision in a particular litigation.

The American system of jurisprudence is a common law system, with essentially three sources of law – the federal and state constitutions; legislation in the form of statutes, ordinances and regulations; and case law, or precedent, the body of written decisions issued by the courts. Legislatures are considered the lawmakers and the courts the interpreters of the law; but as a practical matter, judicial interpretation of a statute or constitution can itself become a form of binding legal authority.

No litigation is decided in a vacuum in American courts. Each is decided on the particular facts presented but, in the interpretation and application of the law, the court is guided by precedent. Judges look not only to the relevant statutes or sections of the penal code, but also to prior decisions of the same and especially higher courts. The higher the court, the greater the weight accorded its decisions. An appeals court decision is binding on lower courts within the same system, but can itself be overturned by the ruling of an even higher court. Decisions of lower courts are not binding on higher courts, while decisions by courts at the same level are are taken into serious account.

Relying on precedent does not mean that all cases are decided in exactly the same way as previous ones; it simply means that the legal principle enunciated in one case provides an example or an authority for resolving similar cases. Each case is decided on its own facts, and a court may conclude that a prior ruling was incorrect or because of different fact patterns or circumstances the ruling is not binding on the case at hand. Litigators must be prepared to spend a lot of time doing research into both statutory and case law.

The rules of procedure and evidence

Substantive law – for example, contracts or copyright or criminal law – provides the foundation of a lawsuit, the underlying legal theory for a party's cause of action or, in a criminal proceeding, the prosecution's charge. Another body of laws governs the actual conduct of a lawsuit. The mechanics for commencement and prosecution of a case, including when and how it may be started, what information must be provided, the circumstances under which claims may be joined or dismissed, what testimony can and cannot be introduced at trial – these are found in the rules of procedure and evidence – what many non-lawyers might consider "technicalities."

Far from being irrelevant or merely bureaucratic red tape, most of these rules are intended to ensure a fair trial and due process for the parties involved. A solid grasp of such technicalities and the reasoning behind them is essential to successful litigation. A lawyer unfamiliar with the codes of civil or criminal procedure won't make a very good litigator, since a failure to adhere to procedural or evidentiary rules can mean the dismissal or loss of a case despite any underlying merits.

State and federal rules of civil and criminal procedure govern every stage of litigation, from the pleadings (the initial documents that get a lawsuit going), to motion practice (written requests asking the court to make certain legal rulings), to pre-trial discovery (efforts to obtain relevant information from the opposing side), all the way through the trial, judgment and appeals process. Because most cases do not actually get to trial, a litigator will likely spend a good part of her time handling pre-trial work such as drafting and reviewing pleadings, motion papers and discovery documents.

In both civil and criminal litigation, the case is supposed to be decided based on the evidence presented. Much of a litigator's job involves the gathering and preparation of evidence for admissibility at a trial. Evidence can include the testimony of witnesses, experts and parties; physical evidence such as the weapon used in a crime or financial documents in a commercial litigation; as well as any facts that both sides have agreed upon. Not all evidence uncovered is admissible – evidence deemed irrelevant, unreliable, privileged (like communications between attorney and client or priest and penitent) or unfairly prejudicial might be excluded.

Unlike the dramatic courtroom scenes familiar to Perry Mason fans, there are actually few surprises when it comes to evidence. This is because before every trial the parties participate in discovery. Each side must supply the other with requested (and relevant) facts and documents, in order to give the other side opportunity to prepare and respond. It is extremely rare, therefore, to have surprise witnesses or to introduce documents that the opposing counsel hasn't already seen. Even if an attorney only discovers the evidence during the trial, he will be obliged to submit it to opposing counsel – and usually give her additional time to prepare an adequate response – before he is allowed to bring it into court. The discovery process is vital to both civil and criminal proceedings and can often facilitate a settlement, depending on what is unearthed.

Litigators work in a court system with many branches, levels and varying interpretations of the law. All lawyers are also officers of the court and as such have obligations not only to their clients but to the Constitution of the United States. In seeking the most favorable resolution for their clients, they must also adhere to the rules of professional conduct.

Psst...
Need a Change in Venue?

Use the Internet's most targeted

job search tools for law

professionals.

Vault Law Job Board

The most comprehensive and convenient job board for law professionals. Target your search by area of law, function, and experience level, and find the job openings that you want. No surfing required.

VaultMatch Resume Database

Vault takes match-making to the next level: post your resume and customize your search by area of law, experience and more. We'll match job listings with your interests and criteria and e-mail them directly to your inbox.

Types of Litigation Practice

CHAPTER 3

Civil Litigation

There are as many kinds of civil litigation practice as there are areas of law. Some lawyers are general litigators, while others specialize in a particular field.

Corporate litigation

Most corporate litigators work at large law firms. Corporate litigators may make the big money, even right out of law school, but make no mistake – they work hard to earn it. A corporate litigation associate usually works on complex civil litigation frequently involving large sums of money. The larger the firm, the bigger the case and client, and the more money at stake.

The subjects of these large firm civil lawsuits might involve stock prices and the transfer of securities, breach of contract, shareholder actions or corporate misconduct. To the public and some lawyers, many of these cases might just seem, in the words of a first-year attorney at a multinational firm, like "one giant corporation suing another." But as an associate working on one of these litigations, you'll find that each one has its own intricacies. In a complicated case, there will likely be a large team of lawyers. A junior associate might be assigned to a very small element of the case. You might have the opportunity to write a memorandum to the senior associate or partner on a particular issue, to interview a witness or to engage in extensive research of a particular legal topic. "You're going to do a lot of research in the beginning," says one senior associate.

It is equally likely that you will participate in the dreaded document review or document production. Document production occurs during pre-trial discovery, when the opposing side requests certain documents in the possession of your firm's client. A copy of each document must be turned over to the opposing counsel. In large cases, this can mean producing copies of hundreds of boxes of relevant documents. In a document review, the associate (usually more than one, and often with the help of paralegals) reviews the documents that your firm has requested and the other side has produced. Either of these tasks can take hundreds, perhaps even thousands, of hours.

A corporate litigation case might last years without ever going to trial. "I've been [at my firm] for four years," notes one corporate litigator, "and I don't think I've been even close to going to court." In fact, the goal of many firms is to avoid court as much as possible. Litigators at big law firms spend most of their time in pre-trial preparation: drafting motions and memoranda for the court, dealing with discovery issues, researching and writing legal briefs, preparing witnesses and occasionally negotiating settlements. At smaller firms, the cases are often less complex and the issues clearer because companies frequently turn to smaller law firms to avoid big-firm fees. The litigators in these firms may have more responsibilities and a little more free time than their big-firm colleagues, but often also have smaller support staff and fewer resources.

Do Your Homework

If you are considering corporate litigation – or financial litigation of any kind – then here's a bit of insider advice: read *The Wall Street Journal* every day. Even if you have a business degree, you might not be able to understand all of it. But it will get easier as you persist, and you will learn one of two important things. First, if you keep at it, you will get a sense of the companies, the terminology and the complexities of the business world. Second, if you can't bring yourself to read the *Journal* for more than a week or two, or find yourself completely baffled by it, then maybe corporate litigation isn't the right field for you. The business world, after all, will be the subject of your practice, and if you can't understand it – or find it mind-numbingly dull – then you will probably find a corporate litigation career both frustrating and boring.

Personal injury and other tort lawyers

A tort is a legal wrong – an unintentional or intentional injury to person or property. Tort lawyers represent plaintiffs or defendants in litigation involving such claims as defamation, wrongful death, negligence, product liability and sexual harassment. Plaintiff attorneys usually seek a sum of money as compensation for their client's loss or injury (compensatory damages) and, for egregious conduct, their suit might include a claim for punitive damages as well, an additional sum intended not to compensate the plaintiff but to punish the wrongdoer.

Many plaintiffs' attorneys in personal injury and other tort cases do not charge an hourly fee but instead take a percentage of the final judgment (assuming they obtain a successful result) known as a contingency fee. Some large law firms specialize in tort defense, representing insurance companies or corporations against product liability or other mass tort claims. Tort cases, like corporate litigation, can stretch on for years. The class action lawsuits that inspired the films A Civil Action and Erin Brockovich involved environmental or "toxic torts," based on claims that the corporate defendants' contamination of the environment resulted in injuries to hundreds of plaintiffs.

Intellectual property

Intellectual property attorneys include entertainment lawyers who represent musicians and artists, patent attorneys who work with new scientific achievements and trade secret lawyers who protect their company's secret formulas and manufacturing methods. An intellectual property lawyer has many opportunities for litigation. Although intellectual property itself may be intangible, the rights of ownership can be bought, sold, transferred and infringed, just like other property rights.

Intellectual property attorneys advise clients of trademark and copyright issues in order to prevent litigation and they represent clients before administrative agencies or in civil court against alleged counterfeiters. Litigators might specialize in certain kinds of intellectual property rights. Patent attorneys, for example, often have scientific backgrounds. Other lawyers focus on copyright issues, which protect not only books, but also musical lyrics, movies and artwork. A growing number of intellectual property attorneys handle "new media" issues involving Internet law, computer programs, telecommunications and multimedia. Finally, some corporations hire intellectual property attorneys as trade secret litigators. The manufacturers of Coca-Cola, for example, work with trademark attorneys (to protect the name and usage of the phrase "Coca-Cola") as well as trade secret attorneys (in order to protect the "secret ingredient" that gives Coca-Cola its distinctive flavor). Many intellectual property attorneys have additional degrees in their field of expertise. "In patent litigation," says one intellectual property attorney, "you pretty much need a science or engineering degree. You can't really get away with not having one."

Environmental law

If the environment is one of your passions, then you might have a future in environmental litigation. There are environmental regulations at every level of government and environmental litigators have specialized knowledge of local, state and federal regulations. Environmental litigation is often complex, technical and time-consuming.

Environmental lawyers provide legal services to every sector of the economy improved by environmental concerns. Some lawyers work for or with government agencies to uphold regulations and bring action against industries that violate pollution or other environmental safety laws. Other environmental attorneys work with businesses to ensure adherence to regulations, thereby preventing such lawsuits. Environmental litigators represent clients before government agencies as well as in courtrooms. Private attorneys keep abreast of recent litigation and advise their clients of regulatory changes that affect their businesses. Environmental lawyers might also work with conservationist groups or the Environmental Protection Agency to bring about legislative change. Many environmental lawyers have a strong background in chemistry, biology or engineering, which allows them to distill often complicated scientific issues for their clients and juries.

Family and matrimonial law

Most states have a separate family court with jurisdiction over divorce actions, custody suits, adoption proceedings and other family-related matters. Some attorneys work in a general family law practice; others work only within a particular area, such as divorce law or juvenile crime. Generally, these lawyers work for firms that specialize in matrimonial law or start their own firms as solo practitioners. There are plenty of opportunities for litigation in this field, even though family law attorneys and their clients would often prefer to avoid court.

Matrimonial law includes both divorce hearings and issues of child custody. This field can be extremely challenging and emotionally draining, as two people in a once happy couple now become legal adversaries. A matrimonial lawyer fights for such rights as alimony, child visitation and support, and an equitable division of marital property. Matrimonial attorneys need a sharp eye for financial matters, as well as a solid knowledge of children's law. Some lawyers charge a set fee instead of working by the hour. Some divorces are handled quickly and merely involve the filing of forms. More complicated cases involving large sums of money, disputes over children, or allegations of abuse or infidelity can drag on for years. A divorce lawyer must be a tough negotiator who nonetheless manages to keep the sanity and emotional well-being of his client in sight. Sadly, there is no shortage of work for divorce attorneys.

Some attorneys deal exclusively with juvenile law. Any person under the age of 18 who commits a crime is considered a juvenile delinquent. However, the closer he is to 18, the more likely he will be tried as an adult. Attorneys who specialize in working with juveniles assess their clients' backgrounds and home environments as well as prepare legal defenses to alleged crimes. "Sometimes it wears you down," says a public defender with experience in juvenile law. "You see kids who are so close to the edge and you want to give them another chance. But their home environments are so bad – you don't know if you can really help them from where you're standing."

Family court also encompass other child-related issues such as child abuse and neglect. Attorneys who handle such cases also work with social workers and children's support services. Some attorneys are former social workers themselves or have advanced degrees in childcare, child psychology or sociology. The work can be difficult, especially in a system itself often overburdened. Clients might include children with emotional, mental and psychological disorders. The court's first priority is providing a safe environment for children, but its second concern is keeping families together. When these priorities clash, the situation can become emotionally charged and troubling. A litigator entering this field should be prepared for such logisitical and emotional challenges. On the other hand, family law offers opportunities for litigation experience and sometimes a real chance to make a difference in a child's life.

Labor and employment law

When you think of labor lawyers, you might picture tough-talking attorneys working for the Teamsters and other unions. In reality, labor and employment law is a broad and varied field. Some labor lawyers do indeed work with unions, negotiating fair wages and benefits for workers. Other lawyers are employed by the human resources departments of large corporations. Still other litigators work for government agencies like the National Labor Relations Board or the Equal Employment Opportunity Commission that enforce labor and employment laws. The opportunity to litigate as an employment attorney can occur in suits involving racial discrimination, sexual harassment, worker's compensation, employee drug testing or benefits law. Employment litigators and labor lawyers represent clients in civil suits at the state and federal levels, before government agencies or at arbitration hearings.

Because there are so many different kinds of laws governing employment and workplace issues, attorneys usually specialize in a particular area of law –

whether ERISA, workers' compensation or employment discrimination. Management-side litigators might work as in-house counsel or at private firms that specialize in corporate issues. Attorneys representing employees can work in firms, for unions or at public agencies. Employers are usually eager to avoid the cost and bad publicity of a trial, and their lawyers are often skilled at out-of-court mediation and arbitration. In general, both sides in a labor dispute work towards an amicable settlement and some labor lawyers might have very little trial experience. Attorneys who handle other employment-related issues, such as civil rights violations or wage and hour litigation, might spend most of their time in court.

A labor or employment lawyer often works with human resources departments and there is generally a great deal of human interaction in this job. Law firms usually look for some prior litigation experience or experience working with employee benefits or in human resources departments. Whether you're interested in protecting the rights of minorities in the workplace or defending a corporation against unwarranted litigation by terminated employees, labor and workplace law offers ample opportunities for litigation experience.

Bankruptcy

Corporations or individuals unable to pay their debts and looking for a fresh start might resort to federal bankruptcy laws. Bankruptcy attorneys guide their clients through these often complicated laws and proceedings in bankruptcy court. They file the necessary papers and represent their clients in bankruptcy proceedings. Bankruptcy law combines elements of litigation and corporate law, and an eager young lawyer will find many opportunities to gain courtroom experience as a bankruptcy attorney.

Individuals and many businesses file for bankruptcy under Chapter 7 of the U.S. Bankruptcy Code, which governs the liquidation of businesses and assets. Larger corporations may file under Chapter 11, which provides for complicated restructuring and organization. Chapter 13 allows the borrower to pay off his debts in installments without liquidating all his property. A trustee is usually appointed by the government to take control of the assets in question and to investigate the financial status of the debtor.

Bankruptcy lawyers not only interpret bankruptcy laws, but also negotiate with the government (in the case of unpaid taxes) and private creditors. Although bankruptcy law has its own courts and rules of procedure, many aspects of the practice are similar to other forms of civil litigation.

Bankruptcy attorneys take depositions, interview witnesses, engage in legal research, write motions and appear in court. Bankruptcy proceedings are sometimes adversarial, and attorneys defend clients against creditors, prove the dischargeability of a client's debt and determine the status of certain property or debts.

Bankruptcy lawyers often have a good head for business and finances as well as general litigation skills. Many large firms have bankruptcy departments, some law firms focus exclusively on bankruptcy practice and other bankruptcy attorneys operate as solo practitioners. An attorney's work hours and quality of life will depend on the number of cases a firm takes and the complexity of the litigation, as well as the economic climate of the country. "We're usually the busiest department in the middle of a depression," says a bankruptcy associate in a large firm. "Go figure."

Immigration

In the United States, where non-citizens do not have the same rights as citizens, immigration law and the representation of non-citizens is a specialized area of litigation practice, the demand for which is unlikely to slow down in the near future. Immigration lawyers help foreign business people get work visas, process citizenship papers, work with refugees seeking political asylum and represent aliens facing deportation. Most immigration lawyers spend time in the U.S. Immigration Court and at the Bureau of Citizenship and Immigration Services (BCIS) and, as a result, learn litigation skills very early. Immigration laws and regulations change frequently and immigration lawyers must keep up with legal research in order to advise their clients. They often have a great deal of responsibility at a very junior level.

Immigration lawyers tend to work in small firms and often charge set fees rather than hourly rates. Salaries vary by employer; those who work for corporate clients take home bigger paychecks than those who represent indigent refugees. Many lawyers do both kinds of work to keep their practice strong. Some immigration lawyers are solo practitioners who work with particular nationalities. It helps, therefore, to have strong foreign language skills and an understanding of other cultures. Litigators with a healthy immigration practice usually have a huge caseload; it's not uncommon to be managing 30 or 40 cases at once. Immigration is a slow process and one fraught with bureaucracy and red tape. Litigators who work in this field must be organized, able to multitask and have patience with the slow movement of government agencies. It's also especially important for immigration attorneys to have strong ethical standards; their clients are often vulnerable and impoverished individuals who, as non-citizens, cannot bring suit in American courts and might easily fall victim to unscrupulous attorneys.

Other fields of law in which civil litigators practice include antitrust, banking law, insurance litigation, international arbitration, regulatory law and tax law.

Criminal Litigation

Criminal litigators fall into one of two general categories – government-employed prosecutors and private or public defense attorneys.

Prosecutors

Prosecutors tend to come in two shapes: local and federal. A local prosecutor typically works for the county and represents the state in a criminal action against a private citizen. If you watch the television show Law & Order, you see New York County prosecutors depicted in action. An elected official, known in different states as the district attorney, state's attorney or prosecuting attorney, heads each office. A county prosecutor – typically an assistant or deputy district attorney – applies state laws and penalties to those accused of breaking the law. A prosecutor usually works in a particular division or bureau and might specialize in prosecuting a particular kind of crime – for example, sex crimes, arson, homicide, violations against children or organized crime. In the beginning, a prosecutor handles small misdemeanor cases, as minor as jaywalking, avoiding a subway fare or petty theft. If she works on larger cases, she will probably be under the supervision of a senior prosecutor.

Federal prosecutors work for the U.S. attorney's office in a particular federal district. These attorneys are employees of the Department of Justice and enforce federal laws. A federal criminal case can arise where the crime took place on federally regulated property (for example, airports, Social Security offices, veterans' hospitals or federal parks), where the crime is specifically covered by federal jurisdiction (such as mail fraud or racketeering) or where the crime crosses state lines (stealing a car in New York and joyriding in Connecticut, for example). Federal prosecutors, like their local counterparts, can be responsible for a wide variety of cases and often specialize in one division.

Most U.S. attorney's offices require that applicants have at least two years of prior legal experience, but you can become an assistant district attorney right out of law school. The salary for a county prosecutor is significantly lower than that of a federal prosecutor. While the life of any prosecutor can be exciting, it is not an easy job whether you work within the state or federal criminal justice system. "You have to be really dedicated to be a prosecutor," says a district attorney. "There's a whole lot of burnout."

Public defenders

The public defender is the government's counterpart to the state or federal prosecutor. Public defenders work either for the state or the federal government and represent those who cannot afford to retain their own defense attorney. As a result, the public defender often gets the cases that no one else wants.

Public defenders usually get courtroom experience very early in their career. A recent law school graduate who has passed the bar will almost immediately find himself in court defending petty thieves, drunken students and the like. Many new attorneys start at legal aid offices in order to gain valuable trial experience that they might never receive in a law firm environment. The public defender who becomes a private criminal defense attorney often has an in-depth knowledge of criminal law and procedure that his classmates who went straight into private practice will envy.

In addition to rich litigation experience, public defenders can take satisfaction in helping those who don't have the resources to help themselves. "I feel like I'm doing some good every time I go into court," says one particularly zealous public defender. "These are people that don't get the legal help that we give to everyone else. They're at the mercy of the system." Public defenders usually make salaries similar to their prosecutor counterparts and, even though they work long hours, their schedules are typically not as full as fellow graduates who went to corporate law firms. Public defenders face the same challenges as other government litigators, working with limited resources within a bureaucratic legal system.

Private criminal defense

The size, type and practice of criminal defense firms vary – there are those who advertise on subway platforms, those who work for celebrities like O.J. Simpson or Phil Spector, and everything in between.

Criminal defense attorneys usually have a great deal of trial experience, even if their goal is never to set foot in a courtroom. "If you want to be a criminal defense attorney, you'd better be prepared to go to court," says one defense lawyer. "You can't hide from a trial, if that's what's going to happen." No matter what the charge is – from drunk and disorderly conduct to first-degree murder – there is a criminal defense attorney who specializes in it. Private criminal attorneys are usually the choice of those with enough resources to pay the hourly fee; they will likely provide more personal attention than the public defender, with his busy caseload, can offer. Because every criminal defendant is entitled to an attorney, and because people will always run afoul of the law, there will always be work for private criminal attorneys.

It is possible, but rare, to become a private criminal defense attorney right out of law school. Most successful criminal defense lawyers come from either the prosecutor's or the public defender's office. The vast majority of criminal defense attorneys make less money than their corporate law counterparts, unless their area of expertise is white-collar crime.

White-collar crime

Many large law firms have a white-collar criminal defense division. White-collar defense attorneys also work at small firms and as solo practitioners. These attorneys are generally a different batch from the criminal defense lawyers discussed above. White-collar attorneys typically represent corporate clients against regulatory boards such as the Securities and Exchange Commission or against the corporate crime division of the U.S. attorney's office. Unlike crimes such as burglary, murder or rape, white-collar crime rarely includes a physical component. Embezzlement, fraud, price-fixing, racketeering and bribery are all considered white-collar crime. Punishment for those found guilty can include both jail sentences and hefty fines.

In a complicated criminal action against a particular company, almost every director, officer and prominent employee will have his own legal representation. Once these people might have worked harmoniously for the same business, but now they have conflicting interests. "Even though [white collar] is not particularly dangerous, it's still a criminal defense," says one litigator who has been involved in white-collar cases. "You're defending people accused of crimes, and they can end up testifying against their former co-workers, bosses and friends. It can get ugly."

White-collar criminal defense attorneys can often make money comparable to or even greater than those attorneys engaged in large-scale civil litigation. Just as in large civil lawsuits, corporate entities or officers are often willing to spend a great deal of money to stave off criminal penalties.

Appellate Practice

Even after a jury of 12 people or a trial judge has found your client guilty or awarded her thousands of dollars in damages, her case may not yet be over. Some cases can be appealed to a higher court, and you might find yourself drafting briefs and making arguments before a panel of appeals court judges. Issues of fact that have already been decided by a jury or judge cannot be appealed; a question of law, however, may almost always be appealed. A lawyer in an appellate court will neither examine witnesses, nor introduce evidence, but instead rely on the record of the proceedings in the court below. At the appellate level, attorneys argue not whether an offender actually stabbed the victim or whether a company did in fact terminate a difficult employee, but rather whether the criminal defendant received a fair trial and whether evidence of the employee's wrongdoing was properly admitted at trial. If the appellate judges find that the trial judge made improper rulings (for example, by admitting or disallowing certain evidence, or by granting a motion for summary judgment before the case went to trial), the decision can be overturned, the amount of damages reduced or the case remanded back to the lower court for a new trial.

Some litigators handle both trial- and appellate-level litigation; others specialize in either trial work or appellate argument. Both private firms and the government employ appellate attorneys. Appellate lawyers spend most of their time researching legal issues and reviewing the evidence used at trial. They must be comfortable working with the law when the facts have already been decided. Appellate lawyers will eventually submit exhaustive briefs and often prepare an oral argument for the appellate judges. There will be no jury or witnesses, and the judges will interrupt the attorney periodically with questions. Appellate attorneys, therefore, must be strong public speakers and able to think quickly on their feet.

Appellate attorneys working for the state make a government salary, albeit a bit more than their trial counterparts. Private attorneys specializing in appellate cases can make an unlimited amount of money. Most appellate attorneys either have prior trial experience or experience clerking for a judge.

Public Interest Litigation

Everyone wants to do some good, but those attorneys who want to use their careers to help the underprivileged will find a range of public interest legal careers available. As a public interest attorney, you represent those people who do not have resources to hire their own lawyers and handle cases that have the potential for broad political or social reform.

Public interest lawyers provide legal assistance in many areas of civil law, such as domestic relations (family law), health care, landlord-tenant law or consumer protection. A litigator can help a tenant in housing court fight an eviction or represent the elderly in health care litigation. Litigators also work for nonprofit organizations with a specific mission, such as the American Civil Liberties Union (ACLU) or the Natural Resources Defense Council. This kind of lawyer works with non-lawyers (scientists or activists, for example) to achieve the goals of the organization. Many of these litigators handle class action suits, especially when there are too many injured parties for each to file separate actions. Class action suits take place in different legal areas, including product liability or employment discrimination, and the goal of many class actions is to enact broad social reform as well as to achieve results for individual plaintiffs.

The life of a public interest attorney is not easy, and there is a lot of turnover among the ranks. Funding for these positions often relies on membership dues, gifts from individuals and private grants, and salaries are likely to be low. The obstacles to achieving change may be very great and the red tape can literally tie your hands. Nevertheless, public interest jobs can be exciting and highly rewarding. There's nothing like being thrown into the trenches in your first year of practice to build your confidence as a litigator. And those impassioned about social reform will find few better avenues for job satisfaction than working directly to change the law. Even if you don't remain a public interest litigator for long, the experience you will have gained will be invaluable.

There are many kinds of litigators and even in the fields listed above there is room for specialization. The common thread is a familiarity with the rules of procedure and evidence, as well as strong writing and research skills. America's court system offers ample opportunities for litigation and what kind of litigation you choose to practice depends entirely on your inclination, personality and the training available to you. The next chapter takes a closer look at the lifestyles and salaries of litigation attorneys and shows how certain litigators spend their day.

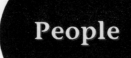

People

Experience

Development

Opportunity

www.blackwellsanders.com

GETTING HIRED

Chapter 4:   The Law School Experience

Chapter 5:   Job Search Basics

Chapter 6:   The Second Summer Internship

Chapter 7:   The Bar Exam and Beyond

Chapter 8:   Leading Employers and Recruiters

The Law School Experience

The decision whether or not to attend law school should not be made lightly. Of course, no graduate degree program should be entered into lightly, but law school is especially demanding (and expensive). If you choose to go to law school, make sure you have solid reasons that will survive that sudden urge after college graduation, when finding a job just seems too hard. Many students go to law school thinking "a law degree will come in handy" in careers other than law. While it is true that a law degree is relatively versatile, don't go to law school expecting to get a generalized degree. Law school is designed specifically to train future lawyers who want to actively practice law, preferably in the state where the law school is located. Few people have the financial resources to go to law school just for the experience.

Law school, at least for the first year, is a full-time occupation. Many schools require that you sign a contract stating that you will not work more than 20 hours a week in order to participate fully in classes. In all probability, you will have classes every day and little choice in your schedule. Tuition will be expensive. The luckiest students have family funding, while most make do with loans of various kinds. A qualified few will obtain scholarships, but law schools generally provide very few of these and, in any event, they are unlikely to cover the entire cost of tuition.

Once you are a lawyer, it will be hard for people to see you as anything else. You might think a law degree serves as a springboard to other careers, but in reality, most employers will see you simply as a lawyer. For those happy in their chosen profession or pleased with the prestige their title commands, that's not a problem. If, however, after obtaining your degree you decide to venture into fields unrelated to law, politics or finance, prepare yourself for a rough transition period. Not only will you have to repay your student loans on a salary likely to be much less than what your former classmates are making, but you'll also meet potential employers who consider you simultaneously overqualified and inexperienced. Although litigation teaches valuable general skills, litigators are not necessarily transitioned easily into other jobs.

So before making the decision to attend law school, think carefully about what it is you want from your education and whether law school will actually give it to you.

The First Step: Getting In

Choosing a law school

Which law school should you attend? In some ways, this question seems simplistic: you want to go to the best law school that will admit you. But what defines a good law school? There are many books about law schools and surveys that rank them, notably the annual issue published by *U.S. News & World Report*, and it is a good idea to review these publications. Even to the uninitiated, some names pop up immediately: Harvard, Yale, Stanford, Columbia. By reputation and stringent academic requirements, schools like these claim to take only the cream of the crop. And a prestigious law school, with its higher profile, might lead to better employment opportunities after graduation than a less well-known school. But there are considerations other than reputation.

Law school is not just for litigators, and no matter where you go your first year will include classes designed to introduce students to the basic principles and subjects of law. In your second and third years, you will be able to specialize in subjects that interest you and courses that teach litigation tactics and skills. If your goal is to become a trial litigator, then you should look at schools with good clinical programs and internship opportunities. If your goal is a more generalized approach to law, select a school that believes in a more traditional and philosophical curriculum.

Admittedly, it's hard to wade through the volumes of press materials each law school will send you. Review the course catalogs, certainly, but also look for statistics about the percentage of graduates who go on to litigation and the kinds of practices they join to get an idea of the kind of training the school focuses on. It's also a good idea to visit the school in person and, if possible, sit in on some classes. "I think it's important to meet with the students at the school," says one recent graduate, "because you get the real facts about what the school is like. Go to whatever mixers they set up for their applicants, if you can."

Another element you should consider is location. Not all of the best law schools are in big cities, but being in an urban setting has a number of advantages. You will have direct contact with many law firms, city agencies and government offices with the resources to hire interns and law students. "Going to a law school in a big city meant that I could have a variety of internships and summer jobs without worrying about housing or moving," says one junior corporate litigator. Many firms also prefer to hire summer associates from local schools. If you have your eye on practicing in New York, for example, it's often a good idea to go to a New York school. You'll be in closer proximity to interview at local firms and some classes (such as criminal law or professional responsibility) may focus on New York state law.

And then there are more practical considerations. Will the school provide housing? If you live off campus, what will your daily commute be like? Are you ready to pick and move alone or to take your family to a new city or state? Can you afford the tuition? Do you share the school's philosophy and emphasis? Is there a particular professor with whom you want to work?

Ultimately, the decision of which law school to go to is as personal as it is practical. Even if it's important to know school statistics and rankings, your choice needs to be a school that will teach the skills you want to learn, in a location where you can live comfortably. This is especially true if you are embarking on a second career and hesitate to uproot your whole life.

Pre-law prep

Unlike medical schools, law schools do not demand a pre-law curriculum. What classes you take in college to prepare you for law school depends very much on your college. Some colleges do offer pre-law classes and you might want to enroll in them, if only to get a taste of what's in store for you. In general, you should take courses that show your seriousness as a scholar. Take courses that encourage writing, public speaking and analytical thinking. Because the study of law is related to the study of government, political science and government courses are useful. "I definitely noticed that poli-sci majors had some advantages when it came to the law school classes," says one former art history major. "I don't think it's a requirement, but if you're not really interested in the government, then you might find the first year less interesting."

Writing courses are particularly helpful, since the more confident you are as a writer, the better your chances of adapting your skills to the particular requirements of legal writing. If you don't take a separate writing course, pay particular attention to the essays you write in government and social sciences courses. Other relevant courses include the study of ethics, philosophy, history and perhaps logic or logical reasoning. Anything that teaches you to formulate arguments and build them persuasively will help you as a litigator.

Your choice of classes will not, however, be the deciding factor in the law school admissions process. One litigator sums up the most important rule of your undergraduate career: "Get good grades. Period." Many law schools claim to look at a variety of elements in choosing their candidates, but the truth is that many students are chosen simply on the basis of their grades and their LSAT scores. Your grade point average counts for a lot, whether you like it or not. True, a 3.4 political science major might initially have an easier time in law school than a 3.8 studio art major, but law schools are partly motivated by pride: they want to keep the average GPA of their accepted candidates high.

Don't despair, however, if you don't have the best grades in the world. If you can, pull them up in the last few semesters of college and in your application essay you can talk about how you became more focused over time. Even with average grades, there's a law school somewhere for you.

The LSAT

For many students, few things are more dreaded than standardized testing, and the LSAT is among the most fearsome tests of all. The Law School Admissions Test is used to evaluate a candidate's verbal and math skills as well as her analytical thinking. The exam can be arduous and exhausting, but it is a necessary element of applying to law school. The LSAT is administered by the Law School Admissions Council four times a year and most schools require that you have taken the LSAT before you apply to law school. The test is roughly three and a half hours long and similar to the SAT – only harder. The test breaks down into the following sections:

- **Logical reasoning** (Two sections, 35 minutes each, 48 to 52 questions total).

  This section tests your ability to dissect an argument. The questions each consist of an argumentative passage of three or four sentences. There is usually a flaw with the argument, and your job is to find out what it is. Occasionally the argument is valid, and your job is to determine the conclusion. This section is pretty dense, so be prepared to do some thorough reading.

- **Analytical reasoning/games** (One section, 35 minutes, approximately 24 questions).

  This is traditionally one of the hardest sections of the LSAT. The best description of these "games" is that they involve logical reasoning of a system of relationships. You'll usually have to draw a diagram to figure out the relationships based on the rules given to you. There are four games and there are five to eight questions for each game.

- **Reading comprehension** (One section, 35 minutes, approximately 24 questions)

As a litigator, you're going to read through hundreds of cases, statutes and memoranda. Reading comprehension is extremely important. This section includes four passages, each roughly 400 to 500 words long and followed by five to eight questions. Your must read each section and be able to answer each set of questions correctly.

- **Mystery section** (One of the above sections, possibly a little different in format)

- **Writing sample** (30 minutes)

The writing sample will be on a topic chosen by the test committee. The essay is forwarded to all the schools to which you are applying, but, according to an admissions official at an accredited law school, their office relies more on the applicant's personal statement than the LSAT essay to evaluate a candidate's writing abilities. The essay is not factored into the total LSAT score. Rather than count on your work being ignored, however, you should be prepared to formulate an argument and present it clearly under pressure.

The LSAT is graded on a matrix which converts the raw score (0-100) to a 120-180 scale. There is no passing score, but it becomes increasingly harder to move up in the matrix. You don't need to get all the questions right in order to get a perfect score, but your score can drop based on the answer to a single question.

There are many courses designed help you to "beat" the LSAT, including Kaplan, the Princeton Review and the LSAT Center Course. These courses teach specific strategies for tackling each section. The LSAT doesn't change that much from year to year, so if you study older tests and practice a lot, you'll improve your chances of doing well on the real thing.

Here are some general tips leading up to and (including test) day:

- **Practice.** If you get used to taking the test, then the real day will seem less intimidating. Find a quiet place and lots of practice tests and take them in real time. You'll get a feel for where you need work and where you need to budget your time more efficiently. "Just make sure you get recent testing materials, as [the test has] changed in the last few years," advises one graduate.

- **Get lots of sleep the night before the test.** It's unlikely that any last-minute cramming is going to make a difference, but getting a good night's rest will. Prepare everything you need – even the clothes you're going to wear – the night before and go to bed at a reasonable hour.

- **Stay calm.** Work at a steady pace and keep an eye on the clock. If you find yourself panicking about one question, then skip it and move on to the next one quickly. "Don't get bogged down," warns one test veteran.

- **When in doubt, guess.** Use a process of elimination: if you can eliminate one answer, then your best bet is to guess among the rest. Don't leave any row of bubbles blank – even if you haven't read the question yet!

- **Read efficiently but quickly**. For the reading comprehension sections, learn to read relatively quickly, gleaning the main points and argument that the author is trying to make. Then go to the questions and see what answers you can eliminate. Don't get slowed down reading the passages too thoroughly.

- **Become familiar with the test formats.** The game section usually has a limited number of game types. Taking a course that enables you to identify the type of question should help you figure out what answers the examiners are looking for. Similarly, the logical reasoning section usually has a limited number of types of questions. If you can identify the type of question, then you're less likely to feel anxious and overwhelmed.

Finally, remember – the LSAT is not a test of creativity. It is a standardized test that follows a strict format. Learning and understanding this format is your best weapon against the test.

Work experience

One of the best things you can do before going to law school is to work in a law firm or at a government agency. Many law firms have internship programs; failing that, you can take a job as a paralegal. In larger firms, paralegal pay can be quite good and you'll get to see how a law firm really works. Litigation paralegals do a variety of jobs, ranging from the mundane (cataloging files, going through documents) to the complex (research) to the downright dull (organizing boxes of documents, alphabetizing, copying). Paralegals are general helpers in the case and, although they cannot practice law, they can become quite adept at identifying and working on legal issues. Paralegals might even be the employees most familiar with the legal arguments and supporting documents in a case. Paralegals see many different kinds of legal documents and whether they're editing or merely copying them, this familiarity will give them a leg up in law school. There is a difference between those who have seen real legal briefs and those who get their knowledge from Court TV.

If law firm life doesn't appeal, consider working at a government agency. Whether it's the local district attorney's office, the public defender's office or the EEOC, government agencies deal with legal issues and the court system on a daily basis. As an intern, there's no guarantee that your tasks will be exciting or that you'll get to see the really interesting cases. And chances are, you'll be working for free. But working with government lawyers, as well as seeing whom they represent, can give you a real sense of what litigators in the government sector do. It's also a good way to get rid of preconceptions you may have gained from the media about the glamorous life of some prosecutors and defense attorneys and the drama of the courtroom.

If you don't have or can't afford to get legal experience, then general work experience is handy as well. You might think that embarking on a second career in law is a step back, but it's a step that a large percentage of your law class is probably taking. Most law schools do focus on undergraduate grades and LSAT scores, but many also consider relevant work experience in their decision-making process. If you don't get legal work experience, make sure you talk to as many litigators as you can find, particularly those who practice in the fields that interest you. They can tell you about their day-to-day experiences and offer you some tips for success.

Extracurricular activities

Most law schools claim to look at your extracurricular activities. While they may not be what clinches your application, outside activities and interests can help you stand out from the crowd. There are some particular activities that law schools like to see and that can also help you develop the skills of a good litigator.

The first is speech and debate. Any organization that encourages public speaking and the formulation of an argument is extremely helpful for those thinking of practicing litigation. "I did speech in high school and in college, and it helped me organize my thoughts. It's handy even when I'm not speaking in public; you learn to approach things from a logical fashion and defend your theories," says one junior litigator. Any good debate team in college will also get you used to thinking and arguing under pressure and developing a clear method of communication.

The second activity that law schools like to see is anything involving public or community service. Volunteering at a local shelter or hospital, organizing clothing drives and even tutoring are all good ways to demonstrate commitment to your community. Community service shows that you are willing to work hard even without monetary compensation and gives the admissions counselor a better picture of those things that are important to you. "I certainly look for community service," says a court attorney in charge of hiring interns. "I like to see that they understand that this isn't a cushy job and that they've done things for reasons other than money."

Finally, any activity that puts you in a leadership position is beneficial. Whether you are captain of the football team or president of your theater club, being in a leadership position shows that you know how to take responsibility, manage large groups of people and rise to the top of an organization. Law schools look for people who will become future leaders as lawyers, business people or politicians, and they tend to look for leadership potential in their candidates.

If you aren't one of those who planned ahead to go to law school and it seems too late to follow some of these suggestions, don't despair. If practicing law is your dream, think about how you might convey that desire and arrange your accomplishments in a really persuasive essay explaining why you should be admitted. Law schools may have an eye on statistics, but they also like to bring together people from all over the country, with diverse skills and interests. When and if you do apply, do so with confidence and enthusiasm, display all your positive qualities and achievements, and show your dedication to the field of law. This will set you apart from the indifferent and lackluster candidate.

The First Year: Be Prepared

So now, maybe you're not quite sure how, but somehow you've been admitted to law school. You're so busy arranging housing and transportation – not to mention financial funding – that you barely have any idea of what you're in for the first year. All you know is that it's rumored to be very hard.

The rumor is true. The first year of law school can sometimes feel like boot camp. You're expected to attend every class and have an organized plan for studying. In addition to participating in class, you'll have to read hundreds of pages of case law, analyze decisions and create outlines that you'll use to study for your final exam months down the line. You might be swept away by the focus and enthusiasm of the other students or lured into the competitive spirit of so many law schools. Whether your goal is to be a corporate litigator or a district attorney, the first step to attaining that goal is to succeed in your first year.

So what will your first year be like? You'll be in a class of people from diverse backgrounds and with varying skills. Unlike most college students, their ages will range pretty widely – some will have come straight out of college, others could be launching a second career. You'll meet former teachers, varsity presidents and fellow students who have children. The most important thing to realize about your classmates is that you are all there because the admissions office felt that you were the most qualified applicants. Suddenly, you're in the room with people who are used to being the smartest in the class. These people will be your study partners, friends, possibly lovers and – because law school finals are graded on a curve – your rivals. It can be an overwhelming experience.

For would-be litigators, the good news, according to many lawyers, is that the first year of law school prepares you more for litigation than for corporate law. You will read cases and more cases and learn from them how to interpret the law as well as how to argue and substantiate a position. Most law schools offer a similar curriculum for the first year. It is important to master the first-year subjects thoroughly because they provide the foundation for your later studies. Typical first-year requisites include:

- **Civil procedure.** You will review the mechanics of civil litigation, the process by which the rights and duties studied in your substantive law courses are enforced, from commencement of an action through disposition on appeal. You will learn the essential elements of a lawsuit including jurisdiction, the rules of pleading, discovery and other pre-trial devices, the joinder of parties and claims, and the effects of former adjudication. For a litigator, an understanding of the procedural issues that govern the stages of litigation is as important as a grasp of the substantive law underlying a lawsuit.

- **Contracts.** A contract is a legally enforceable promise. Sounds simple, right? In fact, the rules governing the formation, interpretation, performance and termination of a contract, as well as what remedies are available in the event of breach make up a very complicated area of law. For litigators, the study of contracts is very important, since many lawsuits arise because one party claims another has breached an agreement. Whether you practice corporate, real estate or product liability law, you will be dealing with contracts in one form or another.

- **Criminal law.** Whether or not you plan to become a criminal lawyer, those interested in human behavior, morality and the role of government should find this class fascinating. You will be introduced to theories of criminal justice, the rationale of punishment and the nature of criminal responsibility. You will also study the basic elements of specific crimes as well as particular defenses like justification, self-defense and insanity.

- **Torts.** This course is essential for those interested in civil litigation and encompasses far more than the personal injury cases typically associated with tort lawyers. Causes of action such as fraud, defamation, invasion of privacy, product liability, trespass, assault and battery all fall within the rubric of tort law. You will study the principles behind the recovery of damages for both intentional and unintentional injury to person or property and the three basic theories of liability: intent, negligence and strict liability.

- **Property.** This course discusses the ownership and rights attached to real and personal property and introduces you to concepts such as possession and adverse possession, present and future estates, easements and covenants, concurrent interests, land use and zoning, as well as methods of conveyance. Many property courses can seem like history classes, since they review centuries-old cases and legal terminology inherited from feudal times.

- **Constitutional law.** Interested in civil rights? This might be your favorite course. It surveys the basic principles of constitutional law and covers issues such as governmental structure (including the sources of federal judicial, legislative and executive powers and federal-state relations), judicial review and constitutional interpretation, as well as the substantive rights granted under the United States Constitution (such as due process, equal protection and the freedoms of the First Amendment). At some schools, students take this course in their second or third year.

- **Legal writing/research.** This class is probably the most practical and useful course for would-be litigators. You will learn the basic skills of legal research, using case reporters, journals and computer research engines like Westlaw and Lexis-Nexis. This course will teach you how to analyze and frame a legal position and how to write office memoranda, court briefs and other legal documents. You will learn how to cite cases properly, using the "Bluebook" – the Uniform System of Citation, the legal world's format for citation in all articles, briefs and papers. The details and nuances of Bluebook form have sent many a student into the depths of despair, but you will eventually master the style. ("If you want to learn the Bluebook," advise some recent graduates, "get on a journal." See below for more on journals.) Some "lawyering" courses also include an introduction to advocacy and oral argument.

The method of grading for the first year of law school can be very intimidating. Most courses are yearlong, which means you will be tested in May or June for things you learned in September. You will have to develop methods of memorization and efficient study techniques. Moreover, in the first couple of months of school, you probably won't be able to discern between vital and trivial information and your early notes will probably reflect this inexperience. It's also common to distribute grades based solely on a final exam, with no midterms or quizzes, which places an inordinate amount of pressure and emphasis on your final exams. Come springtime, you will be juggling five or six finals at once, each of which will determine your grade in that class. Some professors might also factor in class attendance and participation or possibly a midterm exam or paper, but most will rely on the final exam alone. You will have to organize a vast store of information in bite-size pieces, using outlines, index cards, flash cards, even video and audio tapes.

Perhaps unfairly, first-year grades can be even more important than your grades in later years. Judgments about your skills can be made quickly, mostly because employers have little else to go on. Think of this: in February, March and April of your first year, you'll already be interviewing for your summer job or internship. The only thing that your prospective employers will have to review is your pre-law school record and your first semester grades. And you'll be applying for your post-second year summer job – the one that can really make a difference in your career – as early as September of your second year. The only measure these prospective employers will have is your first-year grades.

In addition to being just plain hard, therefore, your first year is also the most influential and pressure-loaded of your legal career. You can, of course, bring up your grade point average over the next two years and still land a lucrative and rewarding job. But in terms of early work experience, how well you manage your first year can make a big difference.

Advice for the 1L

Work steadily

Even if you've been a last-minute, overnight crammer your whole life, that system will not serve you well in law school. There is just too much material for that to be humanly possible. "Don't ever expect to cram," says one graduate, "or leave things to the last minute. You'll drown." Not only will you be memorizing an enormous amount of information, but you will also need to be so familiar with legal principles and reasoning as to be able to use them in a new context on exam questions. You have to work steadily from the very beginning of your first year so that you don't get overwhelmed at the end.

Interact

Set up study groups with serious students and attend them regularly. Go to your professors during their office hours with issues you don't understand. And, as scary as it is, ask questions in class and be prepared to participate. You are not merely being social. Everyone has different strengths and discussing your questions with fellow students can help you understand often complex issues. Yes, it's tempting to see classmates as rivals – why do you want to help others when the tests are graded on a curve? "It's easy to get caught up in the competitiveness, so be careful," says one third-year lawyer. Warns another graduate, "If you're overly competitive, the other students will avoid you like a plague." In reality, a good litigator engages in discussion and a good law student will get used to this at an early stage. Furthermore, law school can be intense, lonely and isolating. A support system can help you keep your sanity in the worst moments.

Don't panic

Law school grades can be brought up in your second and third years. If you feel at sea in the beginning, rest assured – the odds are that most of your classmates don't know what they're doing either. And there's no way to tell who's going to get the best grade. The student who speaks confidently in class may not have the skills to analyze issues on paper, while the quiet, insecure student who takes copious notes and studies on weekends might get the only "A" in the course. So don't spend time worrying about other students' skills – concentrate on your own.

Make use of study guides

There are many study guides available to the first-year law student. You can listen to tapes, study from flash cards, buy professional outlines, attend lectures and even take additional courses. Find what works for you and most accurately emphasizes what your professor emphasizes (she's putting the test together, after all).

Be prepared in class

Do your reading and be prepared to answer questions. Some professors are ruthless inquisitors; others are more interested in fostering general class discussions. Either way, you'll lower your stress level if you are prepared to be called on and give intelligent answers. One litigator offers this tip: "I usually reviewed what I studied right before class, so it was fresh."

Review

You might have done the reading for class and taken good notes, but just because you read or wrote it down once doesn't mean you know it cold. Set aside time regularly to review your notes and previous materials to build up that store of accessible knowledge you'll need to call on for the final exam. Repetition is the key.

Don't get sucked in

Try to keep up with your friends outside law school and engage in some extracurricular activities, even if it's just going to the movies occasionally or playing a game of basketball. The advantage of interacting with your fellow law students is also its disadvantage: you're all in the same boat. Talking about law 24 hours a day can be exhausting and counterproductive; you can get immersed and caught up in your fellow students' panic attacks or intense competitiveness. "I made a lot of friends in law school," says one former law student, "but I lost some friends, too, because I didn't keep in touch with all my friends from before law school." You will likely have more time and feel less pressure in your second and third years and you will be glad not to have alienated your non-law school friends. Escaping from the law once in a while will actually make you a better student in the long run, and it is an important lesson to keep in mind when you actually become an attorney.

The Second and Third Years

Getting through your first year of law school is an achievement you should be proud of for the rest of your life. The good news is that it gets considerably easier from here. After your first summer – which you've hopefully spent at school, an internship or a legal job (see the next section for details) – you will be entering your second year of law school far more prepared to deal with the pressures of being a law student. You can also start making some choices that will help you prepare for a career in litigation.

The first thing you should expect is a considerable lessening of intensity in your law school career. While this has obvious positive effects – less stress, more free time – it also means that the close camaraderie of the first year is gone. You won't be in as many study groups because not all your friends will be taking the same classes. You also won't be isolated from the rest of the school, and many of your classes will be a mix of second- and third-year students. And, because you'll have more going on in your life than law school, you'll also need to be your own motivation to get to work.

Most law schools have at least a few more requirements after your first year, but after those, you're left with a bewildering array of choices for your remaining classes. You don't have to know exactly what you want to do after graduation yet. Many students don't make up their minds about their careers until their third year, after they've taken enough courses and seen enough of the legal profession to make an informed decision. So you can take that criminal procedure course as well as that corporate finance course without worrying that one of them will be wasted.

What elective classes you do take is entirely up to you. But in your academic schedule, as with most of your career, it helps to be organized and plan ahead. You simply won't be able to take all the classes you want, so it helps to have some idea of what your interests and skills are. Here are some questions to consider:

- **Are you taking enough theoretical courses?** You might feel that you've overloaded on theory, but in truth, theory is the foundation for success in litigation practice. Courses in legal thinking and jurisprudence can sharpen your abilities. "In interviews, people are still going to ask about theory," says one litigator. "They want to know that you have a solid foundation in the basics."

- **Are you taking enough skill-oriented courses?** Litigators who know what general litigation documents look like have an advantage over those who don't. Drafting classes, for example, will give you an idea of what kind of papers you'll be preparing as a lawyer and how to do it properly. Courses in negotiation, mediation and advocacy can also provide practical skills you might need in your litigation career.

- **Are you taking enough clinics?** In your second and third years, you can get academic credit for clinics and internships with government agencies and public interest organizations. This is going to be your first opportunity to work with real litigators and figure out where you want you career to go. Many schools can help place you in these positions. "I don't think there's anything more valuable than a clinic," says one federal prosecutor. "Everybody should try to take one."

- **Are you fulfilling your requirements?** Unless you want a particularly dry last semester in law school, you'll need to take your requisites early. The most prominent requirement for nearly all law schools is professional responsibility, which reviews the ethical questions a lawyer faces and the attorney's obligations to society at large. As part of your application for admission to the bar, you will be tested on this material. "The [Multistate] Professional Responsibility Test is a joke," according to one junior corporate litigator, "but you've still got to take the class and pay some attention."

- **Are you preparing for classes that you want to take in the future?** Some courses have prerequisites. If you want to take advanced trial advocacy and argue mock trials in front of real litigators, then you'd better have taken beginning trial advocacy!

- **Can you live with your schedule?** If you're absolutely not a morning person, don't force yourself to take 8 a.m. classes unless you're really passionate about the subject. And if you hate final exams, arrange your schedule to have seminars or other classes that require a paper instead of an exam.

- **Are you satisfying your curiosity?** If you've always wondered about entertainment law or what it takes to be a children's rights advocate, then this is the time to find out.

- **Are you working with professors you enjoy?** A good professor can make even the driest subjects come alive. If you enjoy your class discussions, look forward to office hours and find that a professor's lectures make complicated issues clear, consider taking more classes from the same professor. Plus, "professors are great references," notes one partner at a litigation firm.

- **Are you preparing for the bar exam?** OK, it's years away and not particularly pleasant to think about. But take a look at what subjects are covered in your state's bar exam and see if you're preparing for at least most of them. You've already had a course in property, but what about trusts and estates? You might naturally be inclined to take a course on evidence, but maybe you should think about a class in corporations as well. "There are many classes I wish I'd taken before the bar," says one litigator, "but they just sounded boring in school, so I skipped them. You can get by, but I think the people who actually took wills and trusts had an advantage." You can actually – and will likely – cram for the bar exam over a period of months, but it never hurts to prepare in advance.

Beyond the Classroom

The great thing about law school is that a lot of your real learning will happen outside the classroom. In your second and third years you will have more time and, while you should definitely be enjoying a less frenetic schedule, it's also important for you to take advantage of some of the opportunities your school provides in the form of clinics, journals and other extracurricular activities.

Moot court

If your goal is to be a trial lawyer, then you should consider participating in moot court. Moot court teams prepare and argue issues before a mock panel of judges and enter into competitions with other schools. The teams prepare a written brief and an oral argument for a mock appellate-level court. As a member of the team, you might be assigned to research a particular issue or to write part of the brief. Those who argue in front of the judges present their case as the judges interrupt them with questions and concerns. Tryouts for moot court usually occur in the early summer after your first year of law school (yes, just when you think you're getting a break from school). Typically, you will be assigned or choose a partner with whom you will prepare a brief and argument on a particular subject. The judges will give their recommendations and the current team will help form the new recruits for the upcoming year.

Moot court can be very rewarding but very time-consuming, so be prepared. "I don't know anyone who did moot court and another extracurricular activity. At least, not seriously," says one moot court veteran.

Law review and other journals

Most law schools have a number of journals, each of which deal with a particular area of law. Common topics for journals include international law, entertainment law, environmental law, human rights law, criminal law, urban law, and law and technology. Journals publish anywhere between one to four times a year and contain collections of articles written by notable legal scholars. Your job as a member of the journal staff is to help put each issue together, from the ground up. You may be assigned minor editing duties, fact-checking or office hours. A good portion of your time, however, might be spent "Bluebooking." When articles are turned in, all references to cases must be properly cited. If you're working on a journal that publishes often, you will become a whiz at Bluebooking, able to identify correct and incorrect citations.

As a second-year student, you will probably be as active as you want to be in the journal, but you may not have a title. In your third year, you may apply for positions such as managing editor, articles editor or assistant editor. Your job will be more supervisory and administrative – working with the law school to make sure that the journal has proper support and funding, working directly with prospective authors, assigning second-years to various office tasks and generally managing the journal's publication. Becoming an editor is prestigious and will teach you much about writing and publishing legal work. If you choose not to become an editor, you can still be a member of the journal and contribute in other ways.

Some students contribute a "Note" to the journal. The note is an analysis of a legal issue in the journal's subject. The student must have especially good credentials because the note will be included among articles by prominent legal scholars. In some schools you do not have to be a member of the journal for which you are writing a note. A litigator must have excellent writing skills and publishing a note is both great experience and a prestigious accomplishment. When people look up your subject in Westlaw, they will find your name as a published author.

The competition for journals occurs at the same time that moot court does, in early summer. Each school has a different selection process; typically, you will be assigned one topic to write about for all journals. The journals' editorial staffs will review the submitted essays and the students' grades and, possibly after a group interview, select students for the upcoming year. If you did well on the essay and have good first-year grades, then you may have your pick of journals. Choose your journal based on the subject matter, the staff and the journal's reputation.

The exception to this journal selection process is law review. Each school has a law review which is similar to but by far the most prestigious of any other journal. Most students are invited to join on the basis of their first semester GPA alone. The cutoff varies, but students frequently must be in the top 10 percent of their class. In other respects, law review does not differ from other journals, except that it is far more time-consuming. When you are signed on to law review, you are signed on for your second and third years. And while it is possible for a particularly ambitious student to participate in both a journal and moot court, it is almost unheard of for a student to do both law review and moot court.

Nothing, however, will put you ahead of the pack like law review. Even if your grades slide after your first year (not too much, hopefully), having law review on your resume will give you bragging rights for years to come, and be a huge advantage during the recruiting process.

Clinics

For future litigators, there are few activities more useful and practical than a clinic. A clinical program is a combination of internship and class that will put you directly into the legal world. Clinic opportunities vary from school to school, but there are many common to most schools. Most students in these clinics are placed with government agencies. A criminal defense clinic, for example, assigns third-year law students to clients in need of criminal defense. A prosecution clinic could place students at a district attorney's or U.S. attorney's office to prosecute misdemeanors. A mediation clinic trains students in the skills of mediation or arbitration. Students participating in a family law clinic might assist clients with divorces or handle juvenile law cases. A civil litigation clinic might have students participate in landlord-tenant or small claims court cases. Other clinics focus on domestic violence or human rights or death penalty issues.

You receive academic credit for clinics. You put in a certain amount of working hours at the clinic office or agency and you might also attend a class. Most clinics are thoroughly supervised by working attorneys as well as a professor or two. In these clinics, students are actually practicing law – they can appear in court, write memos, counsel clients, gather evidence and information and, in short, make a real difference in people's lives. It is as close to being a lawyer without passing the bar exam as you can possibly get.

Unlike other law school classes, you can't just sign up for a clinic when you register for your other courses. Most schools require clinic applicants to be third-year students, so you'll probably be applying during the second semester of your second year. You usually must interview with the clinic administrators who will want to talk about everything from your interest in the particular clinic to your grades to your pre-law school life experience. Some clinics are more popular than others, because they provide better legal work experience or are administered more efficiently or are simply better publicized. "The criminal defense clinic at our school had dozens of applicants, but the prosecution clinic had about six," says one litigator. "People just weren't hearing about it." Your competition, therefore, may be fierce or nonexistent. Treat your interview with the clinic administrator like a job interview – prepare to emphasize your strong points and your passion, as well as to explain your weaker points.

It may help to apply for more than one clinic, although some schools place a limit on how many clinics you may apply for. Normally, you are only allowed to participate in one clinic and, truthfully, you wouldn't want to participate in more than one. A clinic is a full-time job in some ways – you are responsible for a case (usually with a partner) and will be working as an attorney. The intensity of your experience can vary, but you will have more responsibility than you have had in your previous years and it can be extremely time-consuming.

The advantages of clinic experience are obvious. When you interview for jobs, you can tell your interviewer that you have already represented a client in housing court or participated in child custody hearings. You can mention a client you kept out of jail or a thief whom you prosecuted. A clinic will help you stand apart from the other applicants who only have theoretical knowledge and no practical experience.

There is, however, one caveat. Don't enter a clinic just to boost your resume and then let your grades slip. While practical experience is important, the sad truth is that nothing will pull you ahead of the pack as reliably as good grades.

Extracurricular activities

With all that goes on in law school, it might seem like too much to get involved in extracurricular activities. But all law schools offer them and they can actually help shape your career. You can use your passion for a particular area of law and help people at the same time. Most law schools have a variety of clubs and organizations. Some are law related – for example, the Housing Law Association – where you can use your growing legal skills to provide assistance to those who need to navigate the judicial system but can't afford to pay for it. You might be able to do some really practical work, like submitting letters or memos to a judge or even appearing in court yourself.

Other extracurricular activities include working with such general community organizations as Habitat for Humanity or cultural groups like the Gay and Lesbian Student Association, the Asian-American Organization or the Irish Law Students. Remember, not everything you do as a law student has to be about law. Employers want to see a well-rounded candidate. While you don't want to overburden yourself, you should get involved in those clubs that speak to you and help you pursue the goals you find important.

Don't, however, join an organization just to put it on your resume. "I don't make decisions based on extracurricular activities unless they're really exceptional," says one litigator in charge of hiring. "We might talk about it at the interview, but that's not what I'm most interested in." Very few employers will place more emphasis on extracurricular activities than on your grades, so be wary of overburdening yourself in this area. In your second and third years of law school, you should follow your interests, explore different areas of law and concentrate on what kind of job you want to apply for when you graduate.

Job Search Basics

CHAPTER 5

You can, of course, choose to use the summers between your school years to relax and have fun, but a wise law student will fill this time with internships or other legal work experience. This is important not only for your resume, but also to investigate the kinds of litigation and legal work you want to pursue after graduation.

You will probably get your summer job after your first year based on one or maybe two sets of grades. Firms, agencies and court offices start the hiring process in February, well before you've taken most of your finals. For many students, your job after your first year will be an unpaid internship. You can work as an intern at a government agency, for a judge in his chambers or even at a law firm. You can, if you like, forget about law altogether after your first year and just go on vacation. It's not recommended, but it's your choice.

The Hiring Process

On-campus interviews

Many law schools have on-campus interviews. During on-campus interviews law firms and government or private agencies set aside one or more days to send representatives to the school to meet with prospective lawyers. Some schools have on-campus interviews all year round, but the season tends to be heaviest in the fall of your second and third years. This is when firms and agencies hire their summer interns. Keep your eyes and ears open to learn about deadlines and procedures for on-campus interviews.

The on-campus interview resembles nothing so much as a cattle call, since some interviewers will see as many as 25 students a day! As a result, your actual time with the interviewer will be strictly limited, probably to no more than 15 minutes, if that. Traditionally, you will be given a list of employers interviewing and will be allowed to submit resumes to a certain number of them. Then the employers will select the students with whom they want to meet and you will be scheduled for an interview. You might have multiple interviews. Almost every on-campus interview will be with a large, general practice firm. The agencies who participate in on-campus interviews tend to be local agencies – your city's district attorney office, for example. The higher your school is ranked, the more employers who will visit and the wider your choices for interviews.

Networking and other ways to get noticed

If you don't get called for many on-campus interviews, don't despair. There are other ways to get an employer's attention; on-campus interviews are just the most convenient. And if you're hoping to work for a small or specialized firm, then you're better off engaging in your own job search. While it might seem at times like there are only 30 firms in the whole world – certainly this is how many law students talk – in reality, there are thousands. The firm that's right for you may not have a large public relations department or might prefer a more intimate hiring process.

If you want to get noticed outside the on-campus interview process, consult the career services office at your law school. Many firms put the word out that they're hiring by informing particular schools. You should also check out the classified ads in legal journals and newspapers. It's not particularly efficient or cost-effective to send out hundreds of resumes to every law firm in the book and you would do better to tailor your search to firms that might actually be hiring. Schedule informational interviews if you're not sure what kind of work you want to do. Your career services office will have alumni and contacts lists of people who will be happy to give you 15 minutes to explain what they do for a living. You'll get good advice and, more importantly, the person you meet might think of you next time there's an opening at her firm.

When all else fails, network! Networking is a great way to expand your options. There are job openings out there, and a majority of them go to people who network with potential employers. Go to your school's social events and legal seminars. Ask your career counselor for a list of alumni who work in the fields that interest you. While you're at it, check out the alumni from your undergraduate college. Everyone you know should know that you're looking for a job. When you are networking, there are a few principles you should keep in mind:

- **Don't ask outright for a job.** Don't mention hiring unless you know that person is in charge of hiring and there is definitely an opening. To ask about potential openings when there aren't any is the fastest way to get the door closed in your face. What you want to do is expand your network of contacts with each encounter. Ask to meet a practicing lawyer to talk about her job or to pick her brains about how best to proceed with your job search. Make it clear that you're not expecting her to line up an interview for you – just give you some advice.

- **Don't be shy**. Ideally, you should be calling your potential contacts, but if you don't think you can manage that, then send a politely worded e-mail. Make sure you introduce yourself, highlight what you and your potential contact have in common and what you would like from them. If you can, meet them in person – people remember faces better than names and phone calls. If you feel bad, remember that you're not trying to freeload. You're offering valuable skills that will be useful to the right firm or agency. And you can return the favor when some young graduate approaches you several years from now.

- **Don't give them your resume**. Unless they specifically ask for it. A resume highlights your best accomplishments, but it is also a way to compartmentalize you. You need to engage the contact in conversation to show them who you really are and what you're looking for. If you do give them a resume, make sure it's at the end of your meeting or a day later, after they've gotten to know you. That way, they'll remember you more as a person than a piece of paper.

- **Be persistent**. Some people will turn you down outright. Others will be discouraging. Just keep going – you'll find more helpful people than unhelpful ones.

- **Ask for other contacts**. At the end of your meeting or in your thank-you note, ask (politely) if your contact can think of anyone else that might be helpful to talk to. This is how you keep networking. If this person isn't helpful, then perhaps his friend or brother-in-law or co-worker might be.

- **Be grateful**. Send a thank-you note or a follow-up phone call or e-mail. Even if this person wasn't especially helpful, make it clear that you appreciated the time she gave you. Courtesy is essential and perhaps this person will think of you if something does come up in the future.

- **Use your referrals**. Always highlight your connection to a potential contact. Write "Referred by…" in the subject line of your emails. Talk about the college you both attended.

Regardless whether you rely on campus interviews or your own job search methods, there are two things that are essential in both processes: your resume and your interview.

The Resume

In all likelihood, you will go through many interviews during your law school career and your resume will change from a general work resume (or one tailored to your previous career) to one that reflects your legal skills and experience. Obviously this may not be possible in the beginning of your legal career since few first-year law students have much legal experience.

Probably the first time that you'll need to polish your resume and send it out will be soon after your first semester at law school, to apply for internships during the summer following your first year. You might also need it to apply for certain classes and programs in your school. It's all right if you don't have legal experience yet; most students don't. Arrange your resume to reflect those skills which will convince an employer that you're on your way to becoming an exceptional lawyer. For litigators, writing and editing skills are very important, as are any managerial or organizational positions you may have held. If you have done community service or been involved in any political activities, make sure to highlight those in your resume. Emphasize any promotions or increase in responsibility in your jobs as well.

A good resume does not go too far back. At this stage in your career you probably shouldn't include your high school grades or activities. Your resume should fit on a single page. It's extremely rare that you will need more than one page, regardless what you were doing before you went to law school. Multiple-page resumes are usually reserved for high-level executives or PhDs with many publications. By the way, although you should certainly emphasize your own publications, list only the relevant ones. You can provide a separate list together with your resume.

Contents

Your resume, at this early stage, should include the following information:

Education

- **The name of your law school and expected date of graduation.** If you have any exceptional grades, list them. If you are involved in any law school activities or hold any titles, list those as well.

- **The name of your undergraduate school and your date of graduation.** Include your major (and minor, if any), your grade point average (if it's high), any scholarships, prizes or awards you may have received, and any relevant extracurricular activities. At this point, the quantity of extracurricular activities doesn't matter as much as the quality. Don't list the school newspaper if you were only there for one semester, but list the drama club if you became treasurer after four years of involvement.

- **The name of any graduate schools or study-abroad programs.** Again, highlight your accomplishments and any notable grades or awards.

Work Experience

- **List jobs that you have had in the last four to six years**. This timeframe is flexible, but it's probably not going to help you to describe high school summer jobs unless they were law-related. An exception to this rule is when you are embarking on your second career and have considerable experience in a particular field. In this case, go by number of jobs rather than number of years – list your last three to five jobs.

- **Don't think that you can impress people by piling on as much work experience as possible.** This will take a lot of space and probably won't add substance to your resume. If the jobs were all in different fields, then it will simply look like you've been wandering through your employment without a plan. If the jobs were in similar fields, then you won't add anything by listing them all. Include the most important ones rather than the entry-level ones, and use the additional space for good descriptions.

- **If you have had varied work experience and many jobs, then you should ask yourself these questions:** What will listing this job say about me as a litigator? Will it show that I can write or hold positions of authority or handle many tasks? Is the organization prestigious or at least well-known? Did I work there for a long time, showing my dedication? Is my supervisor at this job one of my references?

- **Under each job title, you should provide a brief description of your responsibilities and accomplishments.** Use your judgment on what to list and make use of the available space. If you have listed five jobs, you won't have much space to elaborate. If you've only listed two, then feel free to go into more detail for each one. Be sure to phrase your descriptions so that they convey what you actually did. Don't say you were "in charge of" bank deposits, say you "supervised" or "handled" them. Whenever possible, use active verbs to describe your duties.

Miscellaneous Accomplishments

- **You should leave at least a few lines to highlight any special skills you have.** Of particular importance are language skills (be sure to note how proficient you are, and don't exaggerate!) and any special computer skills.

Remember, you're competing with an elite group of people, so use this space carefully. Don't write "knowledge of many computer programs" or anything similarly obvious or vague. If you have special proficiency in anything – you're an awarding-winning chef, a swimming champion or a licensed real estate broker – feel free to put that down. Employers, contrary to popular belief, do want to know something about your personality. This is the place where you can give them an idea of who you are. If you don't have any special skills, it's perfectly acceptable to include a one-line list of your hobbies and interests.

General resume guidelines

Exaggeration

Many applicants exaggerate a little on resumes. Be very, very careful. When you're describing your duties, you'll probably get away with making them seem a little more active, a little greater in scale and authority than they really were. You don't need to be humble when you're writing your resume, and you certainly want to put your best foot forward. By all means, put your duties and accomplishments in the most flattering light. Under no circumstances, however, should you lie about anything! Facts can easily be verified and a lie will, in most cases, immediately disqualify you for the position you're seeking. Don't say that you held a position that you didn't or had responsibilities well above your station. Don't make up accomplishments or exaggerate the length of your employment.

Omission is acceptable sometimes – you don't need to volunteer that you quit your last job because you had a fight with your boss. You can also be a little vague about your length of employment, particularly if a job was some time ago. But you should certainly not exaggerate or lie about your work experience, your grades or anything else. When in doubt, tell the truth or leave it out.

Style

There are different ways to organize your resume. The traditional method is outlined above, listing education, work experience and special skills, usually in chronological order. You can also write a resume that categorizes your experience by skill – for example, organizational, leadership, writing. (You'll still need a separate section for education). Generally, a chronological resume is more traditional for litigators, but if you feel that your skills are better viewed according to subject matter, then by all means feel free to use this format.

Appearance

Your resume is not the place to get creative. Don't try to cram in everything you've ever done by reducing the margins to half an inch or the font type down to 8- or 9-point. Employers have to look at many, many resumes and will not appreciate one that is packed to the limit, making it difficult to read or understand. It won't make you seem more qualified – it will just show that you weren't able to decide what was most important, and neither indecisiveness nor long-windedness is an attractive trait in a litigator. Don't get fancy with the paper, ink or font. Only applicants for creative jobs – fashion editors, graphic designers and the like – should play with unusual paper or dramatic visuals. Your paper should be a neutral shade of white, off-white, light gray or beige, and your ink must be black. Select a font that's easy to read and use it throughout your resume.

Proofread

If you are listing things with bullet points, make sure that they are evenly spaced. If you have subject headings in a 14-point font, make sure they're all the same size. Punctuate consistently; if half of your job duties end in periods and the other half don't, it will look sloppy. Check your verb tense as well; it's no good saying that you "supervised" interns in the same job that you "manage meetings." Any job that you are not currently engaged in should be described in past tense. Have a neutral party review your resume for anything you might have missed.

Theme

Take a look at your completed resume and see if you can find a theme. Did you do some writing at every job you've had? Or were you always working with people? You don't want to seem skilled in only one area, but if there are some consistent themes in your job experience, it can make you appear more organized in your career than you really are! (You'll also have something to consider for interviews). If you have a particular career goal – say, to be a trial attorney – emphasize everything you've done that will show that you have the skills, experience and interest to be a top trial lawyer.

Update

You will need your law resume to be ready at any given moment. Make sure you update your resume to include your latest activities, references and special awards.

Professional advice

Your law school will probably have career counselors who can help you format your resume and fix things that you didn't even notice. Get career guidance from anyone who looks at resumes or does hiring on a regular basis.

You can even hire someone to do your resume professionally; just make sure it still reflects who you are.

Sometimes your resume is the only thing people will know about you. You want it to be as close to perfect as you can possibly make it.

Mastering the Interview

Interviews can be the most nerve-wracking experience in law school, especially if they're on campus. Suddenly you have exactly 10 minutes to set yourself apart from the other 20 candidates this interviewer is seeing that day. It's not easy, but, like most things, becoming a good interviewee is something you can learn.

Before the interview: Prepare

Handling any high-pressure situation is largely a matter of preparation. Even the most relaxed, laid-back law student can be blindsided by a question or an issue she didn't anticipate. If you're surprised at the interview you can become flustered. The whole process can snowball – with each difficult moment you end up increasing your anxiety. To help reduce your stress level, consider these questions before each interview:

- **What do I want this interviewer to know about me?** Namely, what are your strengths? Always refer to your resume for this; it's what employers see first anyway. Whether it's your grades or your community work or your summer at a law firm, be prepared to expand on your experience. "Someone told me to have a couple of anecdotes to tell," recalls one litigator. "Some story that shows off your strengths. It really works – people remember that." Be as specific as possible; you want to set yourself apart from every law student who says something generic like "I'm good with people."

- **What are some of my weaknesses?** Yes, interviewers still ask this corny question, so be prepared. If you didn't get top grades your first semester, be prepared to give a logical explanation for why you're still the best candidate around. Have your grades gone up? Did you have a personal tragedy? Your answers here should be brief and simple. Don't make excuses. Acknowledge your mistakes and try to find something positive about each one.

- **What do I know about this firm?** When you're looking for a job, it can seem like you have nothing else on your mind. Sometimes you feel like you'd be grateful to get any offer. This is NOT the attitude you want to convey. With every interview, you must have some idea of whom you're interviewing with and what they're looking for. "I would never go into an interview without at least logging on the web site or asking other students who might have worked for them," advises one junior litigator. At the very least, you can do a little research about the firm's practice areas – talk to other criminal lawyers, for example, if you're meeting with a criminal defense firm. Memorize a couple of salient facts about the firm or the practice area and be prepared to talk about them.

- **How much time do I have?** You'll probably have a scheduled period of time and it won't be much. Prepare short, interesting answers and explanations. You can plan them down to the word, but be prepared to deviate from your format so you don't sound too memorized.

- **Do I seem confident?** No interviewer is going to hire you if you don't act like you really believe you are the best candidate for the job. This does not mean arrogance. This simply means that when you talk about your strengths, you are persuasive. When you talk about your weaknesses and try to put a positive spin on them, you believe – or act like you believe – your answers. You can be confident in your abilities and humble at the same time; just present yourself as someone who's been lucky in her opportunities and always tried to do the best she can.

There are other, practical details you need to consider. Make sure you have a couple of good interview suits in black, gray or navy. The more conservative the firm, the more conservative your attire should be – don't get carried away with fanciful fashion! This is another area where you should do the research. As surprising as it may be in the 21st century, some conservative firms still frown upon a woman in a pantsuit. Do you know if you're interviewing with one of those firms? Women should make sure they have a few spare pairs of pantyhose, and everyone should have a solid pair of interview shoes that have been nicely polished. "Job aren't handed out according what you wear, but it does tell the interviewer something about you," says one litigator who participated in on-campus interviews.

Once you've got the right look and the right preparation, you're ready to go to the interview. Still, there is one more thing you can do. It helps to go through some kind of dry run or dress rehearsal, and many schools offer a mock interview program in which you can go through a practice interview and see what issues you still need to work on.

At the interview: Be involved

The interview might seem like an ordeal in which you have no power. After all, the interviewer is the one who asks the questions – he's in charge of what's going to happen, right?

That's only partly true. If you've done your preparation, you have some things you want to emphasize about yourself. You should never let an interviewer go without knowing your strengths. This doesn't mean that you blurt them out at the end. Think of the interview as more of a conversation. Let the interviewer lead with his questions, but find a way to be yourself as well.

The initial interview will be brief, especially if it's a campus interview. Here are some tips for approaching the interview:

• **Be early.** Getting there early will allow you a moment or two to compose yourself. You don't want to seem out of breath and you'll get a chance to review some of the things you've prepared. Do not be late. "Lateness is unforgivable in most cases," warns one interviewer. If you think one interview is going to make you late for the other, try to work something out with either the interviewer or the recruiting coordinator at your school. This is the only acceptable reason to be late since, given the number of students who interview on-campus, it may not be possible to reschedule.

• **Answer the interviewer's questions.** Always. Never brush over something that the interviewer seems interested in. If he wants to know about your experience as an extra on Law & Order, talk with him about it, whether you think it's relevant or not.

• **Listen.** When the interviewer is speaking, really listen to his questions or concerns. This sounds simplistic, but often when we're nervous, we tune out the other person's words because we're so busy preparing our next answer! "I want a student who can stay focused on the issues, and I notice when they don't answer my questions," says one litigator involved in the hiring process. In fact, it's good to get this skill down now. Anyone – especially clients and judges – can be offended when they feel they're not being listened to.

• **Ask questions.** If you've prepared well, you should already have questions about the firm. If you've been doing your homework, you might even have some questions for this particular interviewer. You can also ask for explanations of subjects you don't understand. Don't fumble your way blindly if you're confused by the interviewer's question. "Questions show involvement," notes one attorney. The interview isn't only a time for the firm to get to know you, but also for you to get to know the firm. Do you really want to make an uninformed decision?

- **Emphasize your strengths.** This is very important. It's rare that you won't have an opportunity to speak about your interests and accomplishments. Be alert to any chance the interviewer gives you to speak freely. You should have something to say, whether it's a story, an anecdote or a quality you'd like to emphasize.

- **Be human.** This sounds ridiculous, right? But interviewers make their decisions based on more than your resume. You want to be the kind of person with whom they'd like to work. Even though the interviewer won't be making the hiring decisions alone, she will be the one to recommend, and maybe even fight for, you. Share some of your interests or show a sense of humor. You can even reveal some personal information about where you're from – briefly. You don't want to get carried away by this tactic, but at the very least, try to be relaxed. According to one interviewer, "I make allowances for nervousness, but I do look at the student and think, 'Would I enjoy working with this person?'" Remember, the interviewer is human, too!

After the interview: Follow up

Send a thank-you note to the interviewer as soon as possible. That means, of course, that you should know the interviewer's full name; pay attention when she introduces herself. If, for some reason, you missed her name, you can send a thank-you note to the firm's recruiting division. A simple note saying that you were happy for the opportunity to meet with them and that you look forward to their response will suffice.

Callbacks

Unfortunately, your on-campus interview (if you have one) is just the first step. If the interviewer likes you (and your grades and your resume), then you will probably undergo a marathon of mini-interviews known as the callback.

First: congratulations! It may take days or a couple of weeks for you to hear about your callback, depending on how busy the firm is and how many applicants they have. But once they've called you, it means that you impressed the interviewer enough to stand out over your (considerable) competition. Now it's time for you to meet the firm and go through another round of interviews to see if you've got what it takes to work there.

The callback will most likely take place at the firm. If you live in the same city, this won't take more than a few hours out of your life. If not, then the firm will probably fly you in and put you up in a nice hotel. Either way, be sure to have a conservative, clean suit and polished shoes ready. You will meet a succession of partners and associates – usually about four attorneys, but possibly more. You might be invited to a firm outing or lunch with one of the associates, especially if you've flown in from another state. Because you'll be meeting more than one person, you MUST arrive on time. Each interviewer has set aside some time to meet with you – from 15 minutes to an hour. They are all very busy, and if you arrive late, you'll knock everyone off schedule. (Unfortunately, this does not mean that they will be on time; be prepared to have your interviews shuffled or shortened, depending on what comes up).

When you arrive, you will be handed something that looks suspiciously like a dance card, with a list of three or more names. These are the people with whom you will be meeting. Most of the time, you will meet with a combination of partners and associates, many in the department in which you've expressed interest (litigation, for example, or bankruptcy).

The callback interviews start in one of two ways. The first method is to sit you in a conference room and have the interviewers visit you one by one. The second is for you to go from office to office. Don't worry about getting lost; generally, the person who just interviewed you will accompany you to the office of your next interview. The length of each interview will vary, but be prepared for the whole callback to take as long as four or five hours. Make sure you sleep and eat well beforehand, and wear comfortable shoes. The associates and partners will ask you about yourself, your legal career and your interests. They will probably have access to your resume and, sometimes, your grades. Some interviewers take the process very seriously and will have read the materials before you arrive. Others are more casual and may just want to chat. The best advice is to go with the flow and be prepared to answer questions on a variety of topics.

At the end of the process, you will meet again with the administrator or attorney who met you in the lobby. While you may get a job offer right then and there, don't be worried if you don't. It might take a week or two for you to hear back from the firm. The callback can be draining, but the fact that you were invited for more interviews means that the firm is seriously interested in you. Stay calm, review the interview tips above and reward yourself afterward!

Psst...
Need a Change in Venue?

Use the Internet's most targeted

job search tools for law

professionals.

Vault Law Job Board

The most comprehensive and convenient job board for law professionals. Target your search by area of law, function, and experience level, and find the job openings that you want. No surfing required.

VaultMatch Resume Database

Vault takes match-making to the next level: post your resume and customize your search by area of law, experience and more. We'll match job listings with your interests and criteria and e-mail them directly to your inbox.

> VAULT
> the most trusted name in career information™

The Second Summer Internship

CHAPTER 6

Whether or not you spent your first-year summer doing something law-related, it is important to have a legal job after your second year of law school. Employers might overlook a largely non-legal resume from a first-year student, but they're less likely to do so for a law school graduate. Hiring for the summer after your second year can start as early as September of your second year and go into the second semester.

Large law firms usually have a fixed number of second-year law students they want to hire for their incoming class. Depending on the economy and the kind of year the firm is having, a law firm might offer permanent positions to many – sometimes all – of their summer class. That means that if you get your dream summer job at a firm with a relatively lenient hiring process in the beginning of your second year, you might have your future career already mapped out, after just one year of law school!

Nonetheless, although firms try to fill the summer class with people to whom they anticipate offering permanent positions, nothing is set in stone. You still need to do good work as a summer clerk. Even if you have a strong work ethic and the determination to turn your summer job into an offer, your first experience in a firm or government agency can be an overwhelming one. For one thing, law firms will probably pay you a pro-rated first-year attorney's salary (which can work out to be more than $2,000 a week!) and expect you to do real legal work. There will also be many social activities and a temptation to spend most of your time at expensive lunches and after-hour cocktails. For a law student who's never tasted the firm lifestyle, this can be incredibly intimidating. But if you're organized and levelheaded, your second summer job can be one of the most rewarding experiences of your life.

Big Law

If you've been hired by a law firm, congratulations! You will spend a good portion of your second year getting to know the firm, through cocktail parties, introductory lunches and seminars. Large law firms spend lots of money on their summer class, and most want you to have a good time while you get familiar with the firm and the legal world. As your second year of law school winds down, your summer employer will ask questions about the kind of work you want to do. Don't be afraid to be a little uncertain. At larger firms, you will have the option of doing a variety of legal work. You'll also spend a lot more time with the firm's associate attorneys and the other members of your summer class, some of whom you might end up working with. Take advantage of the opportunity to interact with associates; ask as many questions about their practice and the firm itself as you can think of.

When your summer begins, you'll probably go through a series of orientations in which you will learn about the firm's work and hiring policies, its departments, seminars and social activities. These events might flood you with a huge amount of information and advice. But remember that the firm is just trying to make your transition easier. Don't take it too seriously, but don't ignore the help being offered either.

In the largest firms, you will probably share an office with one or more summer associates. You will have all the equipment that practicing lawyers have, from the basic (desk, computer, supplies) to the technical (computer passwords, security cards). You will probably also share a secretary with other associates and partners. In short, you will be paid and treated as a professional, so be sure to act like one. You may have a formal dress code, which means suit and tie for men and suit and pantyhose for women. Few firms are so formal as to require that their female summer clerks wear skirts, but this is something that you should learn ahead of time.

The summer program at most firms is filled with fun activities. You will be wined and dined at some of the city's best restaurants. You may, at bigger firms, go to a play, a baseball game, a formal event and maybe even a country club retreat. You might feel pressure to go out and to take advantage of the firm's generosity, particularly during cocktail hours. Do feel free to enjoy yourself, but use your judgment and always keep the long-term goal in mind. Firms want someone who will not only be a good attorney and mix well with colleagues but also represent the firm well. If you spend extravagantly and come in daily with a hangover, it will be noticed.

The work

The summer can be unsettling for many students as they discover that law school is not lawyer school. You will be thrown into work you haven't trained for and might suddenly feel that law school should have been more practical and less theoretical. The good news is that most summer associates feel the same way and most law firms know this. You aren't expected to do brilliant legal work – if you show enthusiasm, organization and common sense, you'll begin your summer well.

You should have given the firm some idea of the cases you're interested in and will probably have your first assignment within a few days of your first week. Like most litigation attorneys, you will be assigned to one or more cases and will report to the associates and partners. If you requested work on a white-collar crime case and end up on a patent litigation, don't take it personally. Chances are, this won't be the only case you get to work on and you'll be able to move on to other cases later. "We try to accommodate all our summers, so not everyone can get what they want," says one litigator involved in the summer program. "We also have cases that urgently need staffing. Maybe you won't get your dream case now, but we'll make every effort to make sure you get close to it."

Billing

You will learn the concept of billable hours. This might be the most tedious part of the job, but it's also crucial to the firm's ability to make money. Like any other attorney, you will record the time you spend on any one case, so the firm can bill that time to the client. If you work on more than one case, which is quite possible, you will have to keep track of how much time you spend on each one. You will be required to turn in monthly timesheets, but many firms recommend that you do them weekly. There is nothing more frustrating than trying to remember what you did 30 days ago, and trying to reconstruct your schedule from memory can also result in faulty billing.

Training, mentors and seminars

Now that you have your first case and know how to bill it, the work begins. How hard you actually work will be up to you and the firm you've chosen. Use other junior attorneys as a guide; while you probably won't work as hard as full-time associates do, you want your own efforts to seem proportionate. In terms of getting a job offer, you really can't work too hard. On the other hand, you don't want to burn yourself out either. You'll have to find a compromise that works for you. If the work threatens to overwhelm you, don't forget that large firms have many resources. You'll probably have a mentor assigned to you, a litigation attorney who has volunteered to mentor a summer associate. Occasionally, a mentor may have misjudged her schedule and won't be unable to spend quality time with you. There is no harm in asking for another mentor or simply taking the initiative and mingling with other associates.

Take advantage of any help that's offered – whether you don't understand the securities case you're working on or need guidance for Westlaw research. And, though gossiping is generally a bad idea, by interacting with the firm's lawyers, you might be able to learn what partners are good to work with and which ones handle the kind of work that you're interested in.

In addition to all the social activities, your firm will probably offer more formal seminars and training classes. As you become more enmeshed in your summer experience, it may be tempting to skip these classes, but remember that they're offered for a reason. These classes will teach you legal principles, research techniques and, most importantly, how this particular firm works.

Research

The summer is your first real chance to work as a litigator. A substantial amount of your work will probably involve legal research. This will not necessarily be like the research you've done for law school papers. A likely scenario is that an associate will call you with a question: "What is the procedure for filing a Rule 12 motion in Delaware?" or "What are the statutes of limitations for fraud in these 13 states?" You will log on to Westlaw or Lexis-Nexis or go to the firm's library and research the question. You will want to be as thorough as possible, but you will also want to be fast – there's a partner waiting for an answer to this question. You probably won't know all the legal issues of the case (few people besides the partner will) and you will have to stay focused on your one question and avoid possibly interesting legal distractions along the way.

Sometimes you'll be asked a question that doesn't have an answer. While this experience can range from frustrating to nerve-wracking, there's a good reason behind this. A partner or senior associate may be contemplating a course of action and wants to confirm that it's not possible before eliminating it. Your job is to leave no stone unturned so that she can move on to another theory.

Writing

As a summer associate, you may get to write an internal memorandum, take notes during a client interview or review court transcripts. Don't be afraid to ask a lot of questions. It's always a good idea to show your drafts to your mentor or another attorney, preferably someone who knows the case. It's also wise to ask for samples of previous documents. If you can see how other attorneys have approached a research memorandum in the past, you'll have a better chance of structuring your own document properly. In a large law firm, litigation attorneys are not required to re-invent the wheel. Your firm's database will be filled with prior legal complaints, form letters, memoranda, briefs and motion papers, and you will probably have access to them all. No one expects you to know how to write a brief from scratch, and many court motions follow an established format. Make use of the computer database – if you're working for a particular attorney or on a particular motion, see what was written before. It can prove a valuable guide and show you what is expected of you.

Moving around

While you might be focused on litigation, the firm might encourage you to try your hand at some bankruptcy or real estate. Even if you're determined on a litigation career, the summer can be a good opportunity to test the waters in other fields. You might surprise yourself with a sudden interest in corporate law and it's better to find that out now, before you start working permanently in one department after graduation. There isn't any stigma attached in trying out different departments when you're a summer associate, and if you do end up back in litigation your time in other departments won't cause the partners to question your dedication.

Balancing your schedule

Unlike full-time attorneys, summer associates usually work a 40-hour week. The firm isn't interested in overwhelming you with work; they merely want you to get a taste of how the firm operates and what it's like to be a litigation associate. However, if you're needed in a big case you might find yourself working 50- or 60-hour weeks as a summer clerk – or, conversely, with three or four dead hours every day.

Even if it appears that some summer associates glide easily through their work with minimal problems, don't get wrapped up in comparisons. It may be tempting to gossip about your work and to judge yourself by what other summer clerks tell you, but remember, they don't make the hiring decisions. You need to focus on making the people you work for happy.

The trick for getting work done as a summer associate is not much different from handling the workload for any litigation attorney. Be organized, work steadily and make to-do lists. Learn to prioritize by asking questions of the people you work with about what's important and what can wait. Find a full-time litigation associate who manages to keep her workload under control and ask for her secrets. As a summer, you are just learning the ropes and it can't hurt to have positive role models.

Additionally, as a summer associate, you will have the challenge of balancing the demands of your work with the temptations of the firm's summer program. Some of your fellow associates may take three-hour, three-martini lunches at the city's finest restaurants and then go out to a ballgame in the evening. While the main question is whether they get their work done (and some resourceful summers do manage to do so, even with that schedule), this lifestyle is exhausting and not particularly conducive to getting an offer. Part of the summer process is impressing upon the firm that you are serious about litigation and your work. If it appears that you're only at the firm to take advantage of expensive lunches and free sports tickets, then they might not be so eager to extend an offer of permanent employment.

The offer

Summer associates are usually subject to a review halfway through the summer. This may make you nervous, but it can also be helpful in gauging what you're good at and what skills you still need to learn. The review is an opportunity for you to speak up as well. If you've had a bad experience with an associate, a partner or a member of the support staff, you can mention this to your reviewer; but remember, it's always smarter to be discreet and levelheaded. If you're too emotional, people may think you have a personal problem and take your complaints less seriously. The review is also the time to ask for a particular kind of case or to get a better idea of what more the firm can offer you. Don't forget that any criticism is meant to be constructive and don't take it too personally. If the reviewer forgets to mention what you're doing well, ask him!

Attitude, in fact, plays a key role both in getting your work done and in getting an offer. You are now a professional and you should act like one. Partners are experienced attorneys who have been at the firm for at least eight or nine years and very busy people. They are also your bosses, so treat them accordingly. The decision to offer a summer associate a full-time position usually involves talking to many people who know you and with whom you have worked. There are always some politics involved in selecting which summer associates are to be offered positions, but you'd do better to spend your time working steadily and being discreetly social than to play the office-politics game.

Remember, getting a summer associate position means the firm is interested in you, but it doesn't mean that you have to be equally interested in the firm for a long-term position. You will be surrounded by people who enjoy the advantages of big-firm life and it may be easy to forget that there are other great litigation jobs out there. If you find yourself struggling or are just generally unhappy, maybe law firm life isn't for you. Do the best that you can with the resources you have and when your third year begins, start investigating other options. You might be happier at a different large firm, a smaller firm, a boutique practice or a government agency. Better to discover that now, rather than spend years trapped in the wrong job.

Government Positions

Some students spend both their first and second summers as government interns. Legal internships are available in virtually every branch of the government. While they will probably pay less than law firm clerkships, the money can occasionally be supplemented by fellowships from law schools and private agencies. A government litigation job during the summer can be a rewarding experience, particularly for those interested in working for the government after graduation.

Government litigators face a variety of challenges, including small budgets, minimal resources and red-tape bureaucracy. "Whatever firm you're at, you probably have more resources than we did," notes one litigator at the Federal Deposit Insurance Corp. Even if government jobs can be trying, they attract some very skilled litigators. Some lawyers believe that government litigators are sorely underrated. "I don't think there's any difference between the talents of a government litigator and a litigator at a private firm," says a senior FDIC attorney. "In fact, I think government litigators are much more resourceful."

Whether you're looking for a government job at an internship level or after graduation, and whether it's with a federal agency or your local prosecutor's office, there are some characteristics (in addition to grades) that government employers look for.

- **Commitment.** "The salary is significantly lower [than private practice], so we want people who have very strong reasons for wanting the job," says one employer.

- **Resilience.** "The conditions are not always great at government jobs," according to one court attorney in charge of hiring. "I look for people who are unfazed by the lack of resources."

- **Strong communication skills.** A government job involves interaction with people from all walks of life. You need to make yourself clear both in your speaking and in your writing. "I look for a good writing sample, first," says one court attorney. "It doesn't have to be brilliant, but I do want to see that the applicant can write clearly and simply."

- **Genuine interest in social service.** Government employers don't want to think that you're applying for a government job as a safety measure or because you didn't get the firm job of your dreams. Give them real reasons why you want to work for this agency.

- **Knowledge of the field.** If you're applying for a position at the district attorney's office, you need to have a strong grasp of criminal law. Generic knowledge isn't enough; the interviewer will probably ask you specific questions pertaining to your state's criminal law.

You will also need good grades, a confident manner and the stamina to endure multiple interviews. A government interview should be treated just as formally and respectfully as a law firm interview. Be as professional as possible!

Judicial Clerkships

Overview

One kind of government position available to law school graduates is a judicial clerkship. Graduates can clerk with a federal or state judge at the trial or appellate level. Judicial clerkships are quite prestigious, federal clerkships more so than state. Law clerks must commit to a term of one or two years. Some clerkships are so prestigious that law firms and government agencies will allow you to defer permanent employment with them until your clerkship is finished.

Federal clerkships

The application process for federal judicial clerkships has become more streamlined in recent years. Career centers may advise qualified students to apply to many, many judges at once (75 is not an unreasonable number!). Anyone can apply for a federal clerkship, but your chances aren't great if you aren't at least in the top 25 percent of your class. Your other activities and journal experience can also make a difference.

The time to apply for clerkships is right before your third year. By Labor Day, you should have your cover letter, your resume, your writing sample and your references mailed. Don't worry – you won't have to stamp 75 envelopes! Some schools have a system that electronically generates multiple applications from your materials and then sends them out.

Your law school's career center will have a listing of judges all over the country who have clerkship openings. The Administrative Office of the U.S. Courts also has a Federal Law Clerk Information System web site (https://lawclerks.ao.uscourts.gov/) that includes a searchable database of federal clerkship vacancies nationwide. But you will probably only get the most basic information – name, location, deadline, address – from your school's career center. For the real information, you'll have to talk to the counselors or, preferably, alumni who have worked for the judge.

When deciding where to apply, do not rule out a judge simply because his courtroom isn't next door to your law school! Clerkships in certain areas – such as the Northeast corridor or other urban areas – may be more prestigious, but this makes them exponentially harder to get since everyone wants them. Federal law is national in scope, and a federal clerkship in Alabama is still a federal clerkship, which means your Chicago law firm will be duly impressed. And you won't even have to pass the Alabama bar to clerk for a judge there. You should consider any region where you think you can live for one or two years.

You should begin the application process as early as possible so that your materials are ready by September. Your writing sample should be thoroughly proofread and free of any errors. The same goes for your cover letter. You should also try to include at least three stellar references. You can get letters from attorneys you worked with over the summer, but at least one reference should be an academic one.

If you are called for an interview, you will meet with the clerk for your first interview. Unfortunately, the courts don't have the budgets that law firms do, so if the judge is in another state, you'll be paying for the trip yourself. Obviously, if you've applied to clerk with 75 judges and get 75 callbacks (incredibly unlikely), then you must be extremely choosy about whom meet (unless you have an unlimited bank account and a lot of time on your hands). If you're called back after your initial interview, you will meet the judge.

One crucial way that the clerkship application process differs from the firm hiring process is in timing. Once you receive a clerkship offer, you usually have only one day, or maybe two days, to accept. That's it. You can't shop around for the best offer like you do with firms.

The work

Clerkships primarily involve research and drafting. You will research legal issues for the judge and help draft the opinions. Some judges draft every sentence of their opinions; others will let you do most of the work. You will work relatively long, intense hours.

The upside is that you'll get the opportunity to work closely with a judge, who will be your direct supervisor. You will learn more about the law that you can imagine, become expert at research and perfect your drafting skills. The judge will also be a great reference in the future. Most people feel that clerkships are very rewarding. "Many people complain about firm life," says one career counselor at an urban law school, "but I've never heard anyone say that they regret doing a clerkship."

State clerkships

The application information above applies to federal clerkships, at either the trial level (district court judges) or the appellate level (circuit court judges). If you're looking for a state clerkship, you need to contact the court and probably the individual judge for openings and application procedures. Each state has its own procedures. In addition to appeals court clerkships, some trial court judges might hire law clerks. A state clerkship is less prestigious than a federal clerkship, but it can still work to your advantage, especially if you clerk in the same jurisdiction in which you decide to practice law. For instance, if you're planning to practice at a Florida law firm, they might be suitably impressed with a Florida state clerkship. Such a clerkship will carry much less weight for a New York firm.

Money and more

The salary for federal clerkships is usually around $50,000. There might be some adjustment for quality of life – for example, if you're moving to New York City, you might get a small percentage increase. State clerkship salaries vary, from $30,000 to $50,000, depending on state and location.

If you're already working, don't despair – you can still apply for a clerkship. In fact, you have many factors in your favor. Many judges prefer to work with a clerk who needs less training because she already has legal experience.

Furthermore, you'll make more money – thousands more – than if you accepted a clerkship right out of law school.

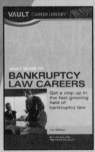

The Bar Exam and Beyond

CHAPTER 7

Overview of the Bar Exam

There is a good chance that the bar exam will be the least enjoyable experience of your entire legal career. Passing the state bar exam is required in order to be admitted as a lawyer in that state. Each state has its own variation of the examination, but most share certain components.

The first component, the Multistate Bar Exam, is the same in every state. It consists of 200 multiple-choice questions prepared by the National Conference of Bar Examiners (NCBE) covering a range of legal topics, including contracts, constitutional law, criminal law and procedure, evidence, property and torts. You will have six hours to answer these questions, in two periods of three hours each. This gives you a little less than two minutes per question. The MBE questions are not short. A question might be several sentences long and each answer will probably also be a sentence or two. In other words, you'll probably need the whole six hours to complete the exam. The District of Columbia and all states except Louisiana and Washington require lawyers to have passed the MBE.

Virtually every state bar exam includes a second, and sometimes even a third, day of essays. Some exams tailor questions to their state's laws (for example, California, New York, Maryland, North Carolina), while other states use the Multistate Essay Exam as their essay section. The Multistate Essay Exam consists of six essay questions spread over the course of three hours. Other states have their own format. Some topics might be familiar to you from your law school classes (like contracts, real property and torts), but others will only ring a bell if you took the course as an elective (such as wills, family law, conflict of laws or corporations). There will be as many as 20 different areas of law that you need to study.

Another component common to most bar exams is known as the Multistate Performance Test. This section is designed to test your lawyering abilities and responses to ethical dilemmas and clients. Not all states use this in their bar exams, and some only use part of it (New York, for example, has only one Multistate Performance question, while other states include more). This section is generally only allotted an hour or two.

Finally, before you graduate from law school, you will probably be required to take an ethics test, known as the Multistate Professional Responsibility Test. The MPRE is a little over two hours long and consists of 50 multiple-choice questions designed to measure your knowledge of ethical standards of the legal profession. The exam is offered by the NCBE three times a year, in March, August and November. If you are not required by your state to take the MPRE, you might be subject to a separate ethics section when you take your bar exam.

All in all, the bar exam is like a two- to three-day legal marathon. You will prepare for it for months and study as you have never studied before. It will often seem that you can't possibly learn as much as you're expected to. Don't despair; as a general rule, more people pass than fail any bar exam and, if you do fail the first time around, you can take it again.

If you already have a job lined up, then your firm may pay for a bar review course such as BAR/BRI or PMBR. Public service and government agencies usually will not pay for this course. Whether it's paid for or not, however, it's highly recommended that you enroll in some kind of course to prepare for your bar exam. There are just too many subjects to cover, many of which you will never have seen before in your law school career, and attending a course regularly will help you develop an organized approach to studying. These courses outline all the requirements for your state's bar exam and review all the legal subjects that may be covered on the exam. You will probably start studying for the bar soon after graduation and take the exam in the summer. Many states offer the exam in late July. Most bar exams are offered at least twice and possibly four times a year, so you can take more time to prepare, if your firm allows it.

Most law firms allow you to take the bar exam again if you failed it the first time. Government agencies such as prosecutors' offices usually won't give you a second chance. Even so, it's quite common for some attorneys to take the bar twice or even three times. Your scores are not cumulative or dependent on each other, and you will only need to pass once.

Test-taking tips the night before

Assuming that you've enrolled in at least one bar review course and have been studying steadily for a few months, here are some last minute-tips for taking the exam.

The night before

• **Pack well.** Get all your supplies together the night before the exam. Put some thought into this. You will need identification, so bring multiple forms of ID if you can. You will likely have an admission ticket as well. Bring it. Other items to bring include:

- Multiple working pens, pencils, erasers and a pencil sharpener
- A sweatshirt in case it gets cold in the testing center and a T-shirt in case it gets hot
- A simple but filling lunch (nothing too heavy) and a couple of non-messy, non-noisy snacks
- Earplugs
- Digital stopwatch (turn the alarm off!)
- Inflatable pillow to sit on or use for your back
- Bottle of water
- White-out (only for emergencies — you usually won't have time to wait for it to dry)
- Kleenex, napkins or tissue
- Some cash, including change for payphones
- Walkman
- Silly, non-legal reading material

• **Review briefly.** If there's something you know you need to work on, spend a few minutes looking the section over. Do not, however, plan to do any intense studying.

• **Relax.** Watch a movie, soak in the bath, play with your dog. If you can, get out of the house – you've probably been cooped up indoors for a few weeks by now. Spending a couple of hours at the bookstore or in the park can revitalize you. Just don't stay out too late.

• **Have a back-up plan for the next morning.** Some people set two alarms; others arrange a wake-up call from a friend or their parents. Map your route to the testing center and plan on hiring a car if you have to. Give yourself lots of time, and then add 15 minutes to that. Make sure you have the necessary groceries for breakfast the next morning. Get your clothes ready and don't leave anything to worry about later. In many states, you can be up to 15 minutes late for the test and still take it. Double check what your leeway time is.

- **Eating and sleeping.** Don't eat right before you sleep; it can make it hard to get up in the morning. Have a good dinner at least two hours before you go to bed. And plan on sleeping at least seven or eight hours.

- **Avoid negative people.** Spend time with people who are going to motivate you and give you confidence. Avoid anyone with last-minute legal questions or their own panic attacks. If you're having a panic attack of your own, call a friend who's not a lawyer or law student to remind you that the world does not begin and end with the legal community.

Test-taking tips: The day of the exam

- **Do not socialize.** If you arrive early, don't interact with other people. What are they going to tell you that's going to make you feel better? After all, they're probably as nervous as you are. Listen to music, read a book, write in your journal or take a (short) walk. Eat lunch by yourself. Talking to other people will probably make you more anxious, especially if they're feeling competitive or panicky themselves.

- **Structure your time.** Take a few seconds to look over each section and see how much time you'll need for each question. Map it out according to your watch. You want to have an idea of where you're supposed to be at all times. You can also decide which questions you want to answer first. (Note, however, that on the MBE there are 200 multiple-choice questions, so you won't have time to skip around too much.)

- **Stay organized and calm.** Read each question carefully and jot down a few notes or an outline for essays. Use subject headings whenever possible. Eliminate unlikely answers and be as neat as possible.

- **Answer all questions carefully.** Don't leave anything blank and be sure to answer each question just as it is asked. Don't get bogged down on tangential details or stray off the topic.

- **Don't rush.** The bar exam days are very difficult and you'll probably want to get out of there as soon as possible. But if you don't want to have to come back, you'll make use of every second available to you now!

- **Beware of snowballing.** One of the worst mistakes people make is letting one error or problem snowball until it becomes a great big problem. Don't let one mistake shake your calm or your confidence. If you think you've messed up one essay question, let it go, and move onto the next one. Don't obsess about a particularly hard multiple-choice question you answered 15 minutes ago.

- **Use abbreviations wisely.** Abbreviations are only useful if you make it clear what they mean. If you find yourself having to make a long list to explain them, then you've used too many.

- **Don't cite cases or statutes.** Unless a case has made a rule of law famous or set a standard, don't worry about citing it.

- **Consider your reader.** A real person is going to read your exam. Write neatly, keep your sentences short and persuasive, and don't get carried away in your statements. Even with all the legal knowledge crammed into your head, you still need to use your common sense.

After the exam

- **Don't go back to the books.** Do not check your answers. It's over. Put your books in the back of your closet (but don't sell them quite yet). Stay away from friends who can't stop talking about the bar exam.

- **Recover** Some people go out to party right after they take the test. Others need some quiet time. The bar exam can be a grueling ordeal, even if you think you did well. Let your mind and body recover.

- **Reconnect.** You've probably been AWOL for a while — reconnect with family and friends who haven't seen you in weeks.

- **Reward yourself.** Pass or fail, you did your best and for that, you deserve a reward. Anything from a new outfit to a vacation is a good place to start.

- **Clean.** Your apartment or house is probably a mess.

And most of all, remember: the bar exam is tough, but most people do pass. If you have studied steadily and put forth a good effort, the odds are in your favor!

Leading Employers and Recruiters

CHAPTER 8

How does Vault come up with its rankings? The first step is to compile a list of the most renowned law firms in the land by reviewing the feedback we receive from previous surveys, consulting our previous lists, poring over legal newspapers, talking to lawyers in the field and checking out other published rankings. This year, our initial list was made up of 148 law firms. We asked the firms to distribute a password-protected online survey to their associates. In total, 11,908 attorneys returned anonymous surveys to Vault. We heard from lawyers in New York, Los Angeles, San Francisco, Palo Alto, Chicago, Boston, Philadelphia, Houston, Dallas, Washington, D.C., Miami, Cleveland, Seattle, Orlando, Phoenix and Atlanta, among many other U.S. locations, not to mention London, Paris and beyond. The online survey asked attorneys to score each of the law firms on a scale of 1 to 10 based on how prestigious it is to work for the firm. Associates were asked to ignore any firm with which they were unfamiliar and were not allowed to rank their own firm.

Think it's easy getting 11,908 associates to take our survey? Think again. Lawyers are busy people, and many are stressed out as it is without having to take 30 minutes out of their day to work on a non-billable project – especially with the increased emphasis on racking up billable hours. Despite it all, an incredible amount of associates came through for us and helped us produce the Vault rankings. Associates, many thanks for your insight and patience.

For the departmental rankings, associates were allowed to vote for up to three firms in their practice areas and were not permitted to vote for their own firm. Associates who identified themselves as corporate attorneys were only allowed to vote in corporate-related categories (securities, business finance, etc.); litigators were only allowed to vote in the litigation category, and so on. We indicate the top firms in each area, as well as the total percentage of votes cast in favor of the firm. (Each associate surveyed chose three firms; the maximum percentage of votes per firm is 33.3 percent.)

Top Ranked Litigation Firms

RANK	FIRM	% OF VOTES	2003 RANK
1	Cravath, Swaine & Moore LLP	8.68	1
2	Williams & Connolly LLP	7.37	2
3	Kirkland & Ellis	7.27	3
4	Paul, Weiss, Rifkind, Wharton	5.40	4
5	Skadden, Arps, Slate, Meagher & Flom*	5.24	6
6	Boies, Schiller & Flexner LLP	4.37	7
7	Davis Polk & Wardwell	4.32	5
8	Wachtell, Lipton, Rosen & Katz	3.63	8
9	Covington & Burling	3.25	NR
10	Jones Day	3.00	10

* Skadden, Arps, Slate, Meagher & Flom LLP and Affiliates
** Paul, Weiss, Rifkind, Wharton & Garrison

#1 - Cravath, Swaine & Moore LLP

Ms. Lisa A. Kalen
Associate Director of Legal Personnel and Recruiting
Phone: (212) 474-3215
Fax: (212) 474-3225
E-mail: lkalen@cravath.com

#2 - Williams & Connolly LLP

Ms. Donna M. Downing
Recruiting Coordinator
Phone: (202) 434-5605
E-mail: ddowning@wc.com

#3 - Kirkland & Ellis

Ms. Norah Faigen
Attorney Recruiting Manager
Phone: (312) 861-8532
Fax: (312) 861- 2200
E-mail: norah_faigen@kirkland.com

#4 - Paul, Weiss, Rifkind, Wharton & Garrison LLP

Ms. Patricia J. Morrissy
Legal Recruitment Director
Phone: (212) 373-2548
Fax: (212) 373-2205
E-mail: pmorrissy@paulweiss.com

Ms. Joanne Ollman
Legal Personnel Director
Phone: (212) 373-2480
Fax: (212) 373-2515
E-mail: jollman@paulweiss.com

#5 - Skadden, Arps, Slate, Meagher & Flom LLP and Affiliates

Ms. Carol Sprague
Director of Legal Hiring
Phone: (212) 735-3815
Fax: (917) 777-3815
E-mail: csprague@skadden.com

#6 - Boies, Schiller & Flexner LLP

Hiring Partners:
Robin A. Henry (Armonk)
Amy J. Mauser and Carl J. Nichols (DC)
Kirsten R. Gillibrand (NY)
Mark J. Heise (Florida)

#7 - Davis Polk & Wardwell

Ms. Bonnie Hurry
Director of Recruiting & Legal Staff Services
Phone: (212) 450-4144
Fax: (212) 450-5548
bonnie.hurry@dpw.com

#8 - Wachtell, Lipton, Rosen & Katz

Ms. Elizabeth F. Breslow
Director of Recruiting and Legal Personnel
Phone: (212) 403-1334
Fax: (212) 403-2334
E-mail: recruiting@wlrk.com

#9 - Covington & Burling

Ms. Lorraine Brown
Director, Legal Personnel Recruiting
Phone: (202) 662-6200
E-mail: legal.recruiting@cov.com

#10 - Jones Day

Ms. Jolie A. Blanchard
Firm Director of Recruiting
Phone: (202) 879-3788
Fax: (202) 626-1738
E-mail: jablanchard@jonesday.com

Psst...
Need a Change in Venue?

Use the Internet's most targeted

job search tools for law

professionals.

Vault Law Job Board

The most comprehensive and convenient job board for law professionals. Target your search by area of law, function, and experience level, and find the job openings that you want. No surfing required.

VaultMatch Resume Database

Vault takes match-making to the next level: post your resume and customize your search by area of law, experience and more. We'll match job listings with your interests and criteria and e-mail them directly to your inbox.

V∧ULT

> the most trusted name in career information™

V∧ULT CAREER LIBRARY

Legal Recruiter Directory

AMERICAN Legal Search, LLC

100 Park Avenue
16th Floor
New York, NY 10017
Phone: (212) 984-1086
Fax: (212) 880-6439
www.americanlegalsearch.com

Where Lawyers Look for Lawyers

Rhonda K. Singer, Esq., Managing Director
rhonda@americanlegalsearch.com

AMERICAN Legal Search, LLC is a full-service national legal search firm. Before launching AMERICAN, our executive management team founded and built one of the largest privately held legal search firms in North America. From law firm mergers and practice group acquisitions to permanent search and contract staffing, AMERICAN's principals have been serving the legal communities throughout the country for more than a decade.
AMERICAN operates three core business divisions:

1. Assist law firms with firm mergers, practice group acquisitions and expansions into new cities.
2. Placement of associates and partner-level lawyers with law firms and corporations on a permanent basis.
3. Placement of contract (temporary) attorneys for specific projects.

Conduit Recruiting Corp.

145 West 45th Street
8th Floor
New York, NY 10036
Phone: (212) 768-2121
Fax: (212) 768-2821
www.conduitrecruiting.com

Mark P. Arrow
President
Phone: (212) 768-2121
arrow@conduitrecruiting.com

Take this job, and love it !

Conduit Recruiting Corp. is a leading legal recruiting firm that places legal professionals with national and international law firms and corporations. Each Conduit client and candidate benefits from our commitment to personalized attention, customized searches and innovative technology - the cornerstones of our business. We are dedicated to fostering partnerships with our clientele to ensure mutually beneficial matches. With our dynamic client base and access to high-caliber candidates, Conduit connects people to jobs.

The Vault Legal Recruiter Directory is a special advertising section. For information on listing your firm in the directory, contact H.S. Hamadeh, Esq. at hshamadeh@staff.vault.com

VAULT CAREER LIBRARY   87

The PeterSan Group

270 Madison Avenue
15Th Floor
New York, New York 10016
Phone: (212) 981-4500
Fax: (212) 981-4560
www.Petersan.com

THE PeterSan GROUP
LEGAL SEARCH CONSULTANTS

Sandrea Friedman, Esq., Peter Goldfeder, Peter Gosule
Managing Directors
Phone: (212) 981-4500 | E-mail: Petersan@nyct.net

The PeterSan Group places attorneys in all areas of expertise as associates, partners, in-house counsel and general counsel and in business and non-legal positions. We also represent law firms in the acquisition of practice groups and firm mergers. Searches are conducted on a retainer or contingency fee basis.

Our clients include leading law firms worldwide as well as financial institutions, investment banks, consumer product, health care, pharmaceutical, entertainment and other Fortune 500 companies.

We work closely with our clients to establish a comprehensive understanding of the particular needs of every search. We then conduct each search in a highly confidential and professional manner.

The Vault Legal Recruiter Directory is a special advertising section. For information on listing
your firm in the directory, contact H.S. Hamadeh, Esq. at hshamadeh@staff.vault.com

VAULT CAREER
LIBRARY

89

Psst...
Need a Change in Venue?

Use the Internet's most targeted
job search tools for law
professionals.

Vault Law Job Board

The most comprehensive and convenient job board for law
professionals. Target your search by area of law, function,
and experience level, and find the job openings that you want.
No surfing required.

VaultMatch Resume Database

Vault takes match-making to the next level: post your resume
and customize your search by area of law, experience and
more. We'll match job listings with your interests and criteria
and e-mail them directly to your inbox.

ON THE JOB

Chapter 9: A Litigator's Skills

Chapter 10: Litigation Career Paths

Chapter 11: The Role of the Junior Litigator

A Litigator's Skills

Because the media focus on litigation attorneys in dramatic cases (whether real or fictionalized), many college graduates enter law school with preconceived notions of what a litigator is like. They envision tough, hard-hitting lawyers with a flair for the dramatic and the ability to weasel every last dime out of the opponent. They foresee spending a lot of time in the courtroom, arguing in front of a jury and cross-examining witnesses, with verbal flourishes and frequent sudden pointing.

Although some litigators might fit this stereotype, it isn't necessarily the portrait of an ideal litigator. In real life, unlike in television studios, courtroom antics can alienate a judge or jury. Tough talk can decrease the chances of a profitable settlement. And open greed, no matter what Michael Douglas said in *Wall Street*, is never good. "I had a picture of what it was to be a litigator," says one junior associate, "but that picture changed almost immediately. It's less dramatic than it looks, and really detail-oriented."

Indeed, the path to a solid career in litigation is not one of bullying and theatrics, but one of perseverance and flexibility. A litigator focuses on details, on being organized and on satisfying her client's wishes. For a successful litigator, winning isn't everything. Indeed, for most litigators, a successful case never makes it to court, but settles quickly – to the satisfaction of the client, who didn't have to undergo the ordeal and pay for the expense of a trial. Litigators must be able to navigate a complex legal system and represent their clients vigorously and professionally, with minimal invasion into their clients' lives and finances.

This section outlines some of the important traits and abilities of a successful litigation attorney. While not intended to be comprehensive, this list does suggest the skills a good litigator should have at his disposal.

Legal Writing: The Pen is Mightier

Many law students think a case is won or lost in the courtroom. This is far from the truth. Before a trial commences, litigators on each side must flex their writing skills in briefs, motions and other legal documents. All lawyers should be competent writers, but the writing skills of a litigator can be the deciding factor in the outcome of a case. Because writing is not always glamorous, it gets little play in the media. Nevertheless, it is the cornerstone of practicing good law.

Many lawyers go to law school because a teacher or favorite aunt told them that they write well. Once in law school, however, they often discover an uncomfortable truth: legal writing is different from other kinds of writing. Elements of journalistic and creative writing might be useful in legal writing, but when it comes down to it, the essence of a lawyer's prose is precise, lucid narrative and a grasp of the logic of the law. Lyricism and attention-grabbing phrases have less value than a clearly expressed argument in what might appear dry language for a writer used to more dramatic touches. Stylistically, lawyers often stick closely to an outline format, using lists, concise sentences and plain words, in addition to common, often Latin-based, legal terms and phrases.

The litigator must either illuminate an area of law or make an argument for an audience that's likely to include busy judges and clerks who want the attorney to get to the point quickly. Although it's important to engage your reader, a legal document is not the place for creative flights of fancy. "I have to make things very clear, very fast," says a public defender. "I can't get too creative or I'll lose my reader. It almost has to be plain." The facts and the law are the muscle and bones of good legal writing; the argument is the sinew that holds it together. If a prior case is interesting but superfluous, it should not be included. A successful litigator knows this instinctively.

A litigator's writing is either descriptive or persuasive in nature. In an internal memorandum to the supervising partner, a litigator does not need to re-argue their client's case. Her task will likely be to explain a particular rule of law, supported by a great deal of legal research. Such descriptive documents will provide the information necessary for a firm to make decisions about the best legal course of action. A persuasive document, often addressed to a judge, argues in favor of a particular course of action. All elements of the document must be focused on the goal of convincing the reader to take this course of action. "Junior associates need to know when to be persuasive and when to be descriptive. And not just in writing," observes a corporate litigation partner.

Fortunately, legal writing is something that can be taught if you've got general writing skills. A good sense of organization, brevity of phrasing and an impressive vocabulary make a good start.

Legal Research: The Library and the Computer

If you anticipate spending most of your legal career striding up and down in front of a jury, think again. Most litigators – especially junior ones – spend a larger part of their time in law libraries or in front of computers. You cannot rely on a mere argument to win a case; it must be supported by thoroughly researched case law.

Research is the substance of any legal argument. No good lawyer would go into court with just his persuasive skills and a plan of action set in stone. Initially, a lawyer comes up with a tentative approach to solving the client's problem and then sets about researching the relevant law. Junior associates will research each issue and try to find as many cases as possible that support the proposed argument or suggest a viable alternative. When a "bad" case shows up, one that runs against his client's position, a competent litigator will not hide it. Instead, he will try to distinguish that case, to differentiate it from his client's situation or show why it does not govern this case. If that's not possible, he will re-formulate his argument – hopefully before the litigation has gone on too far. Hiding the case would be useless; remember, the opposing party is likely researching the same questions and will probably have found the same case. The last thing a good litigator wants is to be sideswiped in court by a case he either ignored or didn't know existed. Better to have an active defense and be prepared. That is the goal of all legal research.

You might find no case similar to your client's in your jurisdiction, but a case like yours might have been decided in another state. You can argue that it applies to the present instance. But you'll need to know the facts of the case, the relevant laws and the cases that influenced the judge's decision. You'll need to make sure that any cases you rely on are still "good law" – that is, not overruled by more recent decisions or a higher court. While this sounds like enough work, in reality, there probably won't even be a case just like yours in any jurisdiction. (If the law were that easy, there would be less litigation!) So you'll have start the process by looking for a case that supports the argument you're trying to make. Hopefully you'll find something close. If you're unlucky, you'll find something that goes directly against your argument. At that point, you'll have to distinguish that case or amend your argument and start from scratch.

Sound confusing? It's easier when you get the hang of it. Some litigators enjoy this investigation into the law. And there's nothing like crafting an airtight argument for your case. But if the idea of spending hours in front of a computer screen, scouring legal databases for the perfect case, actually gives you the hives, then you might want to think twice about a litigation career. "Maybe 10 years ago, you could get away with mediocre computer skills," says a senior litigation associate at a large firm. "Now you can't. Our firm has a couple of partners who don't have computers, but believe me, they're the exception to the rule. You won't get anywhere in litigation without good computer skills."

Communication Skills: If it Please the Court...

Public speaking is the number one fear of Americans, yet it's one of the most important characteristics of a good litigator. Even before they stand before a judge and jury, litigators need to deal with clients, court staff and opposing counsel in a clear and confident manner. The lawyer must be able to distill complex issues of law for his clients and make a persuasive argument. He must speak well and not use unwieldy language or complicated legal jargon to make his point.

Law students often think that a litigator has an instinct for drama. But in truth, theatrics in the courtroom, or at a settlement meeting, can be distracting and counterproductive. Indeed, talking down to juries, being unduly forceful or melodramatic, or spouting homespun clichés in an effort to seem like "one of the guys" rarely convinces even the most unsophisticated jury member. Professionalism, well-researched ideas, enunciation and a genuine interest in the audience are more important than overblown language.

A litigator should be able to think on her feet, but don't imagine that a lawyer "wings it" in the courtroom. Everything – from an arbitration to a passionate closing argument – is carefully prepared for in advance. The litigator wants to sound natural but doesn't leave anything to chance. Large law firms invest a lot of money for their attorneys to argue in front of mock juries, to see what points are most persuasive and which need more emphasis. Some attorneys have themselves videotaped so they can eliminate speech tics and nervous mannerisms. By the time the lawyer gets before a real jury, she should know her argument cold and be able to convey it persuasively and naturally.

Litigators face the additional challenge of presenting often complex non-legal subjects in a lucid and competent manner. For example, imagine a medical malpractice case in which the plaintiff claims he lost the use of his hand due to the doctor's negligence. The case turns on the doctor's use of a controversial technique. The lawyer must be able to explain the technique (or get expert witnesses to do so), explain how it differs from more conventional procedures and lead the jury through a maze of medical terminology. Even if the lawyer is naturally weak in science, he must learn all the facts and present them articulately and accurately. The same goes for litigators involved in product liability cases that hinge on methods of manufacturing or money laundering cases that might require explanation of complicated financial maneuvers and stock movements. Even in a seemingly straightforward mugging, the lawyer often needs to know many details (the weather, the light, the distance, sightlines, what everyone was wearing, their height and weight) and must somehow highlight the important facts to a jury that's getting increasingly bored over the course of eight hours. It's not enough to know the information; the lawyer must be able to present it engagingly and persuasively.

Even those litigators who never see (or never want to see) a courtroom must have superior communication skills. Partners will want to hear your ideas in a clear manner. Clients need complicated legal issues explained to them simply and without confusing legal jargon. Witnesses must be interviewed, either in person or on the phone. And, of course, there's always the opposing counsel. Lack of clarity or confidence could cost you a case. "I used to do speech and debate in college, but I became much clearer in my speech after becoming a lawyer," says a junior associate. "You're always talking, always explaining things to someone and often, you're put on the spot and have to talk fast."

Organization: First Things First

Lawyers are masters of multitasking. When you've got a deadline for a pre-trial motion and the partner wants to discuss what you've written, do you reschedule your witness interview? When do you talk to the court clerks? What about reviewing those 46 boxes of discovery documents for important information? When does all this work get done?

A lawyer works long hours. Those hours get even longer if the lawyer isn't organized. This is especially true in the earlier stages of your career, when a partner will hold you responsible for the whereabouts of every key piece of information. An attorney must know what jobs have priority over others and make sure that everyone on the case – paralegals and secretaries included – knows what is going on. The course of a litigation case can change in an hour. A damaging witness might appear or the opposing party might settle. Deadlines have to be met, regardless of how many re-writes you must do. Furthermore, without a sense of organization, the workload of a lawyer can become overwhelming, leaving little time for a personal or family life. An unorganized lawyer burns out more quickly than an organized one.

A lawyer must also have an internal sense of organization regarding his arguments and research. Lawyers and those who work with them – judges, clerks, partners, paralegals, witnesses – are often pressed for time. A judge, in particular, wants to hear only your strongest points and the most relevant issues. She will not want you wasting her time with tangential facts or unessential cases. A lawyer must organize both his written and oral arguments with precision in order not to flood others with irrelevant information.

Every lawyer develops his own method of organization, but here are some helpful tips:

Get good advice

In the beginning, it may not be clear to you what is the most important issue on your plate. What you might think is pressing might be the last thing on the partner's mind. Get constant feedback from partners and senior associates about your work schedule and how to prioritize it. If you're a prosecutor with different cases, take your cues from more senior attorneys and ask for advice on how to manage what might be an overwhelming caseload. This is not the time for false confidence – it's better to ask the stupid question now than to be unprepared in court.

Get a calendar

It seems like a simple suggestion, but many lawyers overlook it. Day planners work for some, but having a monthly or weekly planner will give you an overview of deadlines coming up and allow you to focus on what is due, and what is not. Even an important case should be put aside temporarily when you have a memorandum due tomorrow.

Ask for deadlines

When handed a project, get specific about when it's due. Court deadlines are assigned and mustn't be missed, but partners' deadlines are equally important. Yes, they can seem arbitrary and confusing, and yes, every partner thinks his job is the most urgent and the most important. Grumble (quietly) if you must, but get your work done. If you find yourself really overwhelmed, there's no harm in going to the managing partner and asking for some help in structuring your week. Nevertheless, some associates are nervous about doing this. "I'm always afraid that it will look like I'm complaining or trying to get out of work," admits a junior associate at a large firm.

Delegate

When you get a chance, delegate smaller jobs to secretaries and paralegals you trust. You don't have to set up file boxes or alphabetize folders if your firm provides a staff to do it. Government jobs often have interns; if you feel bad asking a college or law student to staple a hundred documents, remember that someone probably made you do it, too. Just give them some substantial work to make up for it later on.

Invest in supplies

Government jobs may not have enough resources, but private firms will have great supply closets. Binders, file folders, desktop organizers – even just working pens – can make your life easier. Find a system, invest in the supplies if you have to, and stick to it.

Keep control of your desk

Having a catchall drawer is fine for some people, but for most working lawyers, it's really a waste of space. Every office product should have a home so when you need it you don't have to go searching. This doesn't mean you need a spotless desk; those attorneys who do have one probably don't have enough work! But if you have five piles of work in progress, make sure that each is sorted, and don't put off the filing until it towers over your desk. Taking a few minutes every day to organize your desk can help you feel in control and even provide a break from all that hard legal thinking.

Make "to-do" lists

Some people love them, others hate them; but virtually every lawyer needs some form of a list of things to do. You can make one at the beginning of the week or (preferably) every morning. It will minimize the feeling of being overwhelmed if you can see exactly what needs to be done.

Start small

If you are prone to procrastination, it's best to start small. Don't expect to tackle huge, unwieldy projects when you're lacking motivation. Take a smaller, more pleasant task and finish it. Or break the larger project into bite-size pieces. Remember, just because you started a day spinning your wheels doesn't mean the whole day is doomed. If you begin with some small project – a phone call, a review – then you can build on that to create some work momentum.

It's Who You Are...

The stereotype of a lawyer is often that of a bullying, brash, take-no-prisoners soldier-of-fortune. In truth, lawyers come in all shapes and sizes, with a range of personalities. Some of the top lawyers are shy and reclusive, but masters of organizing research. Others are more extroverted, finding their strength in oral persuasion. There are, however, certain personality traits that lend themselves to a successful litigation career.

Courtesy and respect

Although a litigator must be assertive and sometimes bold, it is not always helpful to be argumentative. Litigation does not have to be a battle, and winning is not everything. A good compromise, rather than a lengthy and expensive trial, might be in the best interests of both parties. A lawyer who is rude to opposing counsel, difficult to work with or unwilling to provide necessary information is not serving the best interests of his clients. He is just looking for a fight. This is even more counterproductive in the criminal law arena, where district attorneys and public defenders meet often in different cases and rude behavior will not be forgotten. "If somebody screws you in one case, you remember it," says a district attorney. "You're not willing to work with them later when they want a plea for a different client."

Moreover, the professional code of conduct is strict. A lawyer who cuts corners or tries to hide evidence creates trouble for himself and his client – not the least of which is a charge of malpractice or a disciplinary proceeding. Even minor sneakiness – overloading the opposing counsel with irrelevant material, for example – will probably result in bad feelings and possibly some kind of reprimand from the judge. Since she's the one hearing the case, do you really want to get on her bad side?

Attention to detail

A good lawyer is detail-oriented. According to a corporate litigation partner, "The fastest way to impress a partner is to become the 'go-to' associate – meaning, every time we need to verify some fact or detail, we go to that associate. Having an eye for detail can make or break a case." A good litigator at any level believes in thorough preparation, whether for a witness interview or passionate closing argument.

Judgment

A litigator makes the best case he can with the evidence available to him and does not back down in the face of some disagreeable testimony. He also understands the value of a good settlement and doesn't let a desire to win overwhelm his better judgment. He can navigate uncertainty and deal with the unexpected. Above all, he is considerate of his clients, listening to their wishes and explaining complicated issues when necessary.

Assertiveness

Make no mistake, however; the ideal litigator has an assertive, even aggressive, personality. He is not out to make friends, but he's not out to make enemies either. Every strategy may be carefully planned, but the lawyer should not seem dispassionate about his case. A good litigator finds a balance between taking a case too personally (resulting in unwanted stress and counterproductive emotion) and appearing indifferent to the client (resulting in lost opportunities). "A corporate attorney is working with two parties who usually want the same thing, just on different terms," says a corporate litigation partner. "Litigation is an adversarial process. You want to fight hard for your client." You're on your client's side and you want to get everything you can for her, within the boundaries of professional courtesy and ethics.

Frustrations

There is no doubt that being a litigator offers intellectual challenge and an opportunity to exercise your well-honed research and communication skills in the service of a client and with the potential for achieving real justice in a worthy cause. But litigators face some less exciting challenges as well. On a daily basis, a litigator's work is generally much more tedious than glamorous, more likely to involve painstaking routine research and drafting (and re-drafting) and legal "technicalities" than exciting investigative work or dramatic trials. Litigation has its frustrations as well as its rewards, and those considering a career in this field should be aware of some of the daily realities facing practicing lawyers.

Details, details, details

Attention to detail is essential for a good litigator. But an appreciation for nuance and subtlety in the interpretation of a statute or drafting of a contract can at times seem like mere technical gamesmanship. The choice of words and the placement of a comma really do matter in the practice of law, so if you find such detailed analysis and careful drafting "nitpicking," you might want to think twice about becoming a litigator – or any kind of attorney.

An adversarial life

For every litigator who thrives on the challenge of building a persuasive argument and winning the best results for her client, you'll find another who is exhausted by endless negotiations, stubborn clients and the posturing of opposing counsel. Litigators should recognize, and appreciate, the adversarial nature of their practice. Even if most cases eventually settle, you are representing one side against another in a fight, presumably a polite and exclusively verbal one, but nevertheless a battle which each client wants to win (and in which you are a hired gun who may or not be convinced of the justice of your cause). There is, in fact, no guarantee that the side you represent will be right. Few lawyers enjoy the luxury of only taking on cases they are convinced are just.

You might deal with angry, bitter clients in your own office only to face lawyers representing equally angry, uncompromising clients in court or across a settlement table. Moreover, even if you do your best to be civil and on time, you will stumble on rude court clerks, difficult judges and the cumbersome machinery of the judicial system. As a litigator, you'll quickly find out that a lot of being in court is kind of a "hurry up and wait" feeling – you might be on time, but the judge or opposing counsel may not.

Expect more tedium than glamour

Many would-be lawyers are drawn to the profession by the profusion of litigation cases in the news media and on television. Very few litigators will actually be involved in anything so sensational as the O.J. Simpson trial or as ground-breaking as *Anderson v. PG&E* (the class action suit at the heart of *Erin Brockovich*), and even if they are, most of their time is unlikely to be spent in the courtroom or before TV cameras, but rather in front of the computer or on the floor amid boxes of boring documents.

There are, of course, many positive realities about litigation practice. If you like doing research, analyzing statutes, poring over contracts and reading cases; if you enjoy the pure intellectual challenge of constructing a persuasive argument and backing it up with supporting evidence; if you like writing, editing and re-writing and appreciate the subtleties of language; if you like being an advocate, responsible for helping obtain or defend something of value to your client (whether what hangs in the balance is a sum of money, a person's freedom or property, or the right to conduct business in a particular way); if you thrive under pressure and don't care that every case isn't a headline-grabber and never makes it past the paperwork stage – then you might find litigation a truly successful and rewarding career.

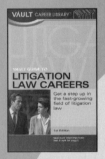

Litigation Career Paths

CHAPTER 10

Those considering a career in litigation have a range of employment options before them. Litigators work in private practice and in the public sphere. They may specialize in a particular field of law or run a general litigation practice. They might concentrate on either appellate work or trial-level practice, handle civil litigation or criminal work. Government agencies, nonprofit organizations and law firms of all sizes are always in the market for good litigators.

Civil Litigation

Mid-sized and large firms

What constitutes a large firm varies from state to state and city to city. A firm of 20 people may be considered large in Monterey, California, while in New York it's considered pretty small. Really large, general practice firms have offices of hundreds of lawyers, with branches not only around the United States but also in Europe, Asia or South America. These large, multi-office firms have substantial marketing and hiring budgets and are the firms most likely to conduct on-campus interviews They also tend to have a higher profile than their smaller counterparts. Most well-known national rankings or surveys of law firms, like the *Vault Guide to the Top 100 Law Firms* and the "NLJ 250" published by *The National Law Journal*, focus on these big firms.

Some large law firms have litigation specialties (patent law, for example), but most are "full-service" firms, offering a mix of transactional and litigation practice, with groups including corporate, intellectual property and real estate law. The structure in these firms is highly organized and extremely competitive. A first-year associate is usually assigned to the practice area of his choice and often has the opportunity to rotate into one of the other departments. The litigation associate usually is assigned to one or more cases, under the supervision of at least one senior associate and a partner.

For the purposes of this section, a firm is mid-sized or large if it has at least 20 attorneys and usually more than one office. Although there are notable differences among mid-sized and large firms in terms of their practice, clients, location and firm ethos, there are certain characteristics many big firms have in common.

High pay

Big firms generally offer the best salaries and benefits packages to graduates right out of law school. The largest firms tend to be competitive with each other in many areas, including compensation, and salaries therefore tend to be very uniform among the largest firms. "I'm making more money than my father," says one associate at a large New York firm. "It's a weird feeling. And I already know what I'm going to be making next year, because it's all pretty much set in stone."

The exception to this rule is the yearly bonus. While firms do keep a close eye on the bonuses paid by their competitors, these figures are not as rigidly set as salaries because bonuses usually reflect the financial success of each particular firm. One firm might offer huge bonuses, while another firm that pays its associates the same salaries but didn't have as profitable a year might offer little more than nominal bonuses. Large law firms in the same city pay almost identical salaries. The average starting salary in a large, general practice law firm in New York is currently $125,000 a year. This figure is sometimes, but not always, lower is smaller cities, perhaps $105,000 in Philadelphia or $100,000 in Atlanta.

Long hours

Attorneys at some big firms might manage to have quite an active social life, but big firms usually expect to get their money's worth from their associates, and few first-year attorneys work from 9 to 5. Associate attorneys at large law firms experience a great deal of pressure to work and bill as many hours as possible, and many firms require a certain minimum number of billable hours each year. Requirements at top firms might range from 1,800 to 2,200 hours. At first, a 2,200-hour billable requirement might seem reasonable – after all, that's about 42 hours a week, and isn't that little more than a "normal" job? But bear in mind that billable hours means ONLY hours that can be billed to a client and therefore can't be anything other than legal work actually performed on a particular case. Lunch hours, casual conversations, organizational work, waiting for a partner to get back to you, training seminars, administrative tasks are not included. If you are very efficient, take no lunches and are lucky in the people you work with and the cases you are assigned, you might meet that 2,200 annual billable hour requirement by working from 9 to 7 every weekday and only five hours every Saturday. And that's not counting time lost on vacation and holidays!

Most new lawyers won't be so lucky or so organized. Litigation cases can be very slow and then get extraordinarily hectic. The bigger firms have showers in the offices, late night car services, cafeterias and a drawer full of menus for ordering in. It is possible to work everyday – including weekends – for several weeks. The simple truth is that the litigation workload in a big firm is nearly impossible to predict but will probably be much heavier than that at smaller firms. "Here's a tip," offers a junior associate in a large litigation firm. "If you're doing litigation in a relatively large firm – say, at least over 50 people – you're going to be working all the time. If I get out at seven, I'm lucky. Some firms like to say that they're more lifestyle-oriented, but I think they're mostly the same when it comes to billables."

Substantial resources

As a law firm grows, it becomes more than a group of lawyers; it becomes a business. The support staff increases in size and skill, and new departments – duplicating, recruiting, computer, public affairs – are established. The law firm's library will probably also expand in size and features. The secretarial staff will be better trained and responsible for more work. The firm will probably hire more paralegals. A lawyer at a large firm, therefore, will probably be able to delegate her non-legal work to other people. Her secretary may do the filing, the paralegals may help in document review, the librarian will aid in research and the duplicating department may make all the copies she needs. All of this assistance is designed to make the attorney more efficient and more focused on her legal work.

In addition to staff, large firms have more money to spend on overheard – like nice offices, extra perks such as gym facilities and a cafeteria, and better computer systems. "I decided to work here for a lot of reasons, not just the money," says one junior associate. "But the perks are really nice. We eat at great restaurants and get cars home when we work late." A law school graduate might get accustomed to this kind of pampering!

Bigger and more complex cases

Large, prominent law firms are where most multimillion-dollar shareholder litigations and class action suits are handled. These firms are able to handle large cases of a complex nature, often featuring many different causes of action, cross-actions and counterclaims. The case might have clients and opponents in different states and might deal with dozens of witnesses and multiple state agencies. Boxes of litigation documents can fill whole rooms at a law firm, and there may be many associates and partners attached to various aspects of each case.

There are both benefits and drawbacks to working on cases this large and complicated. A first-year attorney is probably only responsible for a small portion of a case, and she will have many lawyers to rely on for advice or help. "You might even get to travel, which I really like," notes a junior associate at a large firm. "You're working with different law firms, in different states, and you often need to be on the road to meet with your clients. And when you travel," the attorney adds, "all the expenses are paid." A big, important case can make new law, and the young attorney's involvement in it may be incredibly prestigious.

On the other hand, a junior attorney might easily get frustrated with working only on a tiny piece of a big case without involvement in any of the strategic decisions. Working on a case with so many attorneys can feel impersonal, and client contact might be very limited. Moreover, the sheer volume of work can be overwhelming, and if the partners managing the case are not incredibly efficient, both associates and support staff can become completely bogged down in document review and research issues.

Real experience may not come easily

An ambitious attorney might actually do nothing but document production in her first six months. While her small-firm counterparts are preparing for a trial or actually speaking in court, the junior associate at a large firm might sometimes feel like an overpaid secretary shuffling papers around. Large law firms offer seminars and training, but a new attorney might have to struggle to get practical experience or exposure to the kinds of cases she wants to handle. There's also no guarantee of client contact or sense of camaraderie in a giant, complicated litigation. Large law firms tend to have a regimented approach to assigning work, and sometimes skill and talent is not enough to obtain the really challenging or interesting assignments. The bigger the law firm, the larger and more numerous the cases, and many firms cannot be as receptive as they might like to their young attorneys' desires for real litigation experience.

High attrition and slim partnership prospects

Large firms tend to have very regimented hiring practices. A firm may hire 40 new first-year associates in a given year, yet promote only two seventh-years into partner position. What are the other 38 lawyers in the class expected to do? In all likelihood, they're no longer even there. The attrition rates at big firms is very high. Many mid-level lawyers – attorneys in their third, fourth and fifth years – go to smaller firms where they'll have a better chance of making partner or a better balance of family and work. Some lawyers leave for public service; others go to work as in-house counsel to a corporation.

Those who do stick around in their original firm have a lot to prove, because merely being in a large firm for seven, eight or nine years is usually not enough to make you partner. "It's getting harder and harder to make partner," says one partner at a large litigation firm. "We're making our decisions more carefully than we did during the boom years." You have to have a proven track record of working very hard, as well as positive results in many of your cases. Additionally, the other partners must recognize in you the potential to bring in new clients, since "rainmaking" is one of the duties of a partner. Partnerships in major law firms are incredibly lucrative and considered rare prizes. And, because the current partners decide who will be promoted, the process can also be very political. "You need to get on the right sides of the right partners," says one senior associate. "They're the ones deciding whether you're going to make it."

There are no guarantees early in your career of where you will end up, and sadly, hard work is just not enough. Because of this situation, many litigators treat their time at a large law firm as a relatively short-term opportunity to get a good name on their resume and favorable experience. Those seventh- or eighth-years who do not make partner occasionally become "of counsel." Some firms have other non-partnership track options, like "senior attorney" or "special counsel."

Exposure to other practice areas

Large firms tend to be general practice firms, which means that they have a number of departments outside litigation. One advantage of the many practice groups is that you'll probably have a chance to do a rotation in departments other than litigation. "I started in litigation," says one senior associate, "but I wanted to make sure that was what I really wanted to do. I did a rotation in corporate. It was okay, but I felt like litigation was more interesting, more proactive. I spent a lot of time waiting for people to call me in corporate."

An organized approach to pro bono

A small law firm may desire to do pro bono work, but might not be able to afford to take on more than a few unpaid cases in a year. A large firm, on the other hand, will likely have more resources and greater ability to handle working without a fee. Pro bono cases are a great way to get practical experience in a large firm; they also tend to be litigation-oriented and can offer associates the client contact missing in larger billable cases. Pro bono work can involve a death penalty defense case in Georgia, an immigration asylum case for an Iranian refugee, a divorce case or representation of a charitable organization. The bigger the firm, the more variety of pro bono work, although the energy a particular firm devotes to pro bono matters depends on the attitude and encouragement of the firm partnership. Some firms are more amenable to non-billable work than others.

A Day in the Life of a Corporate Litigation Associate

9:30 a.m.: Arrive at work. Get coffee, make small talk with officemate, and check emails and phone messages with secretary.

10:15 a.m.: Return phone calls and emails. Call senior associate with question regarding yesterday's research issue. Call duplicating to check on document review on white-collar crime case, and put them in contact with paralegal assigned to the case.

10:40 a.m.: Go down to document review room. There are 70 boxes of documents here, but some are out being copied. Review documents with fellow associates, looking for relevant issues.

12:30 p.m.: Associate Lunch in conference room. Lunch/training session is about witness interviews. Take notes and eat roast beef sandwiches. Schmooze with fellow associates about who's working for the most demanding partner.

1:50 p.m.: Return to office. Check emails and continue with yesterday's research issue about statute of limitations in federal court for securities fraud cases. Spend most of the time researching the issue on Westlaw and Lexis-Nexis.

4:00 p.m.: Take a break from the computer and go down to the document review room. Go through witness statements, expert testimony, product promotional materials, statistical data and internal memos to look for evidence of intent.

5:15 p.m.: Return to office and prepare for meeting with partner and rest of team.

5:30 p.m.: Meeting with partner and rest of team. Meeting goes long, but the focus of the research has now changed. Partner would like a memo in 48 hours on this new research issue. Update partner on document review and duplicating process.

6:30 p.m.: Speak with senior associate about organization and approach of new memo and how to research new issue. Check with document review room on duplications of documents. Plan out how much more needs to be done and talk with paralegal about organizing document review.

7:30 p.m.: If you're feeling really motivated, you can go back to the document review room. Otherwise, leave for home, knowing it will be waiting for you tomorrow!

A Day in the Life of a Corporate Litigation Partner

9:50 a.m.: Arrive at work, check emails and phone messages.

10:00 a.m.: Call associates for meeting in half an hour. Look over associate's memo on SEC regulations for shorting stocks after a takeover.

10:30 a.m.: Associates arrive for meeting. Review questions on memo and assign other research issues. Also assign senior associate to prepare for deposition in the next week.

11:30 a.m.: Phone calls to co-counsel regarding trade secret case.

12:30 p.m.: Litigation partners meeting lunch: discussion of upcoming hiring and issues of cases. General news on how the department is doing.

1:30 p.m.: Return to prepare for witness interview on trade secret case. Go over outline that associate has prepared, adding notes and relevant issues. Have secretary double-check meeting time and place and car arrival.

2:00 p.m.: Leave for witness interview with associate.

2:30 p.m.: Arrive at witness interview in midtown. Questions involve what part witness/employee had in acquisition of rival company's product. Conduct interview while associate takes notes. Opposing counsel interrupts with issues.

4:15 p.m.: Call client regarding witness interview. Schedule deposition for SEC cases. Check on associate writing a brief for federal court.

4:40 p.m.: Answer emails and phone messages.

5:00 p.m.: Meeting with associates for pro bono case. (Partner is overseeing political asylum case for Sierra Leone refugees.)

6:00 p.m.: Review of associate's revised memo on SEC regulations. Prepare for document production and assign associates' schedule via email.

6:30 p.m.: Leave for business drinks with president of a small investment firm. (Partners often have to mix business with social activities in order to drum up new business for the firm. This "rainmaking" is a vital part of the partner's job.)

9:00 p.m.: Take the train home.

Small firms

Large, multi-service law firms with high-profile clientele may generate more publicity, but in fact most firms are small and have fewer than five or ten attorneys. Although small firms vary in character and type of practice, they do share some general characteristics.

Greater responsibility and client contact

With only a few attorneys to go around, it's not unusual for a litigator to be the sole attorney on a case. "I went to court in my first year here," says an associate at a small immigration firm. "I have my own cases. It makes me feel like a real lawyer, not just an employee." The small firm attorney can provide more intense, personal attention to each case and be more directly involved in all aspects than is possible in most larger firms.

On the flip side, because of manpower and resource issues, small firms likely won't offer the extensive training that large firms typically provide, and litigators in small firms might be thrown into situations for which they are unprepared. While it's exciting to be in court as a first-year attorney, it's also scary and overwhelming if you haven't been properly trained for it.

Fewer resources and smaller cases

Few small firms will have as many paralegals, secretaries, office supplies, computer resources or manpower as the large national or regional law firms. They will therefore rarely have the resources to take on such big cases as a multistate shareholder litigation where the plaintiff shareholders number in the millions and the amount of paperwork and document review alone would bog down even a large firm. Small firms must be choosy about their cases.

Lower salaries

There are exceptions to this rule, but in general where the cases and clients are smaller, the money made by the attorneys tends to be smaller. Some firms work on a contingency fee basis, meaning the firm only makes money if the client wins the case. The firm will have to weigh the financial risks against the potential profit when deciding whether or not to take a particular case. Salaries for small-firm litigators can range from as low as $40,000 to something in the six figures for more experienced attorneys. Partners, who earn a percentage of their firms' profits, usually take home substantially more money than salaried associates.

Greater flexibility

Small firms hire fewer attorneys than large firms, so new litigators often feel less expendable and more like they have a voice within the firm. Working hours might also be more reasonable. "I don't have nearly the same pressure on me to bill hours as do my friends in larger firms," says a third-year associate at a small firm. Moreover, it may not take as much time or effort to make partner in smaller firms.

Boutiques

Boutique practices are law firms that specialize in a particular field of law, such as labor or employment law, environmental law or intellectual property law. There are small firms specializing in nearly every area of law: domestic relations, health care, labor law, employment, elder care, children's issues, corporate litigation, animal rights, welfare, real estate – you name it. Most specialized small firms are in cities, where there is enough work in that particular area to sustain the practice. "I went to this firm specifically to do immigration law," says an associate at a small immigration firm. "I wasn't interested in doing a broad variety of litigation. I certainly didn't want to do all that securities litigation they make you do in big firms." In less urban areas, a firm might have to become more general and handle different kinds of cases in order to prosper.

In order to become a specialized litigator, you must show passion for the field in work you have done outside law school. For example, if you wish to work with juvenile offenders in family court, it helps to have participated in a family law clinic. Other factors, such as volunteer work or even a relevant undergraduate degree, will help distinguish you from others hoping to enter the same field. "I knew I wanted to work with kids before I even went to law school," says one litigator with extensive experience in juvenile law. "When I got to law school, I had already worked in the children's ward at a hospital and researched the family court system." A prospective labor law firm might look for experience with unions, previous human resources jobs or membership in a labor organization. Environmental attorneys are usually helped by undergraduate degrees in science or engineering. And most employers prefer that their patent lawyers have some background in the sciences. Certain specialty litigators must have additional credentials, on top of their law degree, to practice in their fields. Many tax lawyers have master's degrees in taxation, on top of their JDs, and litigators who want to practice in tax court must apply for admission.

The salary range for litigators in boutique firms depends on the nature of the firm's practice and its location. Most boutiques are smaller than general practice firms and pay less; salaries often start as low as $50,000 a year, but the best and brightest of each firm or practice might well make six-figure salaries. Top litigation or other boutiques might pay as much as some of the biggest multinational law firms. The caseload and work schedule for boutique lawyers vary, but most litigators should expect to work long, demanding hours.

A Day in the Life of an Associate at an Immigration Law Boutique

9:30 a.m.: Arrive at work. Read emails and listen to phone messages. (Immigration lawyers get a lot of correspondence via email.)

10:00 a.m.: Return phone calls and emails.

10:30 a.m.: Prepare letters and documents to Department of Labor regarding upcoming case. Assign forms to paralegal for completion and review later this evening.

11:00 a.m.: Consultation in the office with prospective client for Green Card issues. Get background information for future case.

12:30 p.m.: Lunch at the desk.

1:00 p.m.: Review forms, now filled out by paralegal. Look over case, filling out additional paper work for H-1 Visa applications. Prepare support letters.

2:30 p.m.: Leave for court for Green Card interview for another case. Prepare client for hearing with BCIS*.

3:45 p.m.: Attend citizenship hearing with another client, including client's written examination.

5:00 p.m.: Return to the office. Research regulations for various districts regarding South Korean immigrant case. Prepare for next day.

6:30 p.m.: Head home.

* Bureau of Citizenship and Immigration Services

Solo practitioners

Very few law school graduates start their careers as solo practitioners. The most obvious reason is that in order to start and run your own law firm, you must have a steady supply of clients. Few law school graduates have the connections, let alone the work experience, in order to practice on their own right after law school.

After a few years at a firm or government agency, a litigator might be tempted to move out on his own. First, and most obviously, you must have the skills and the background to market yourself as a private attorney. You must also have the resources to advertise and make your practice known among those people who might need your help. Second, in order to run a private practice successfully, a lawyer must be assured of an income sufficient to support the office as well as her own lifestyle.

Getting the clients is no small feat. Most solo practitioners must deal with an erratic cash flow; sometimes they will be extraordinarily busy and other days see virtually no clients – and no money. A single practitioner must get the word out about his services and somehow distinguish himself from the hundreds of other attorneys offering the same services. He must also be able to offer something that larger firms do not provide – whether it's lower hourly rates, greater personal attention or fabulous litigation skills. Sometimes the number of clients depends on the attorney's connections from his previous job.

The kind of litigation can vary. A small-town solo practitioner might work as a jack-of-all-trades, taking on everything from probate to criminal defense to product liability cases. The nature of his practice may very well depend on how much money is coming in that day. When there's no money, a litigator may have to take whatever case walks in the door. Elsewhere, in larger cities, a solo practitioner might be able to specialize, particularly if he has a great deal of experience in his chosen field and solid connections to ensure a steady flow of clients.

It is almost impossible to estimate an average solo practitioner's salary. An immigration attorney with two years of private practice, no staff and a home office might make just enough money to pay his bills, whereas a labor lawyer with 15 years of experience, extensive contacts at government agencies and in private practice, a staff of five and an office on Madison Avenue might be earning something in the high six figures. Many solo practitioners hire office managers and secretaries to oversee the financial and administrative sides of the practice. This might free up the litigator to concentrate on the law and developing a solid client base, but it also results in other expenses, like rent for office space, salaries for staff, insurance and general supplies.

There are no formal prerequisites to starting your own firm – you merely need to have passed the bar in your state to hang out your own shingle. What you charge will likely depend on your clients and the demand for your services, and what you make can depend on how many late nights you are willing to put in. "I think anyone who does this right out of law school is crazy or at least very idealistic," says one solo practitioner. "I worked for firms for 20 years before I opened up my own firm, and I'm always thinking about where my next client is coming from."

In many ways, solo practitioners are no different from any other entrepreneurs: fiercely independent, with flexible schedules and their own personal work ethic. "I like that I'm my own boss," says one solo practitioner specializing in intellectual property. It can be extremely difficult to start your own practice without previous experience but, because the opportunities to succeed or fail are entirely up to the litigator herself, it might be an option for those lawyers who do not find satisfaction in the more traditional work environment and want more control over their cases.

Criminal Litigation

State prosecutor

There is no single career path for a local prosecuting attorney. Some prosecutors join the county district attorney's office right out of law school; others have had years of private practice. The work of a county prosecutor can be very dramatic and makes good fodder for television shows.

All criminal defendants are considered innocent until proven guilty beyond a reasonable doubt, and it is the prosecutor's job to meet this burden of proof. The first step in any case is the police investigation. Once the police have amassed the requisite evidence against an offender, they go to the local district attorney's office. The deputy or assistant district attorney assigned to the case makes the decision whether to charge the defendant, and what to charge him with. In some cases that might be easy – in the case of a man who broke a window in a Radio Shack and was caught carting off electronics, the charge might be simply be burglary. However, take the example of a man caught standing over the dead body of his wife, with blood on his hands. If he deliberately hit her over the head, he is guilty of murder. If he pushed her violently and she hit her head, he may be guilty of manslaughter. If he was simply talking to her and she slipped and hit her head, he may not be guilty of anything. It is the prosecutor's job to review the evidence, decide what happened and what the charge should be. "You do have a lot of responsibility," says one assistant district attorney, "though sometimes your bosses are the ones deciding where to go with a particular case."

After the charge is filed, the prosecutor works with the police, the evidence and the witnesses to put together a compelling case. They may review the police reports as well as the accused's previous criminal records. A prosecutor might have to present his initial case to the grand jury. This is not a trial – it is merely a forum for the prosecution. to present the case before a grand jury who will decide whether there is sufficient basis to proceed to trial, in which case the grand jury issues an indictment. This is the first hoop a prosecuting attorney must prepare to jump through.

In addition to these duties and knowledge of both the penal code and rules of criminal procedure, the prosecutor must have a strong grasp of the unspoken rules of his criminal court system. Is the judge assigned to the case prone to be lenient towards defendants? Does he require a particular format for his briefs? Is his court clerk helpful or intimidating? Will the trial start on time? These are questions that a good attorney must be able to answer. "Part of my job is knowing one judge from another and being friendly with their clerks and their staff," says one assistant district attorney. "It's not even about the law sometimes, just strategy. You need to be good with people. And good with chaotic situations." And with his huge caseload, a county prosecutor cannot afford to get bogged down with red tape.

Most criminal cases never make it to trial. The prosecutor will meet with the defendant's attorney to work out a plea bargain, in which the defendant pleads guilty to a lesser charge in exchange for a more lenient sentence. A seasoned prosecutor might meet the same legal aid lawyer or private criminal attorney many times in his career and will probably know what to expect from him.

If the case does indeed go to trial, the prosecutor's time will probably be consumed by preparations. A trial is not a minor event and a good attorney will spend hundreds of hours preparing for a trial, focusing on details down to the very last letter of his closing statement. Trials are not won on grandiose gestures in the courtroom, but on how well prepared, thorough and detail-oriented the attorney is. In many serious felony cases, the prosecuting attorney has been known to eat and sleep at work and his social life can stop completely. After all, it's not just the defendant's life that's on the line – the attorney is also trying to find justice for the victim. "When I'm busy, it's ridiculous," says one prosecutor. "Everything stops but the case. You need to be able to give that kind of dedication to a trial without losing your mind. If you can't, then this is not the job for you."

The prosecutor's job is extremely demanding and heavy on responsibility. There is considerable burnout in the offices of big-city district attorneys. Not only is the work complex and often exhausting, but the prosecutor must also deal daily with the bureaucracy of the criminal justice system. Moreover, there are many tough ethical decisions to be made along the way. Public defenders are often asked how they could defend a murderer or a rapist: What if a guilty man goes free? But the prosecutor faces a similar dilemma: What if an innocent man is imprisoned? Sometimes the evidence points in one direction but, as we see often in the news, the real offender gets away. Could you live with the knowledge that out of your hundred cases, at least one defendant may be innocent and in prison for a crime he didn't commit?

Lawyers might find other aspects of a prosecutor's job troubling. How would you feel about accepting a plea bargain from a man who beat an old woman to death? What if he had information on a violent drug dealer that the police have been trying to catch for years? What will you tell the victim's family when the defendant serves 6 to 12 years for manslaughter rather than the 25 to life he would get for murder? "I do a lot more pleas that I thought I would," says one assistant district attorney. "I knew most of my cases would plead out, but it's still hard to do day after day." The vast majority of cases do settle. It may not seem just, but without plea bargains an already overloaded system would grind to a halt.

Yet, working as a state prosecutor can be an incredibly satisfying experience. You will be in court almost immediately and get trial and litigation experience your law firm colleagues will envy. The level of responsibility is high, and you will often have the satisfaction of putting away genuine bad guys and finding justice for victims who have been harmed.

An assistant prosecuting attorney has a large caseload and, while the hours are not quite as brutal as those of a corporate litigator, they can be quite demanding. A first-year prosecutor might also have a varied schedule, including overnight shifts. Starting salaries depend on the city. The starting salary for assistant district attorneys in New York is in the mid $40,000s; in most states it ranges between $25,000 and $40,000. Salary increases are usually determined by the department's budget. Prosecutors with years of experience can stay with the prosecutor's office, head a particular bureau or department, move into private practice or even become judges. Although it is possible to become an assistant district attorney right out of law school, most offices look for some prior litigation experience. Candidates go through a rigorous interview process as well as drug testing, written exams and background checks. You must also be a U.S. citizen and make a commitment to the office for a period of time, generally two to four years.

A Day in the Life of an Assistant District Attorney

9:00 a.m.: Arrive at office, check emails and get files and paperwork for court.

10:00 a.m.: Arrive at court for multiple issues, including an arraignment for a burglary case, hearings for drug possession cases, money laundering case and attempted murder case. Speak with court clerks while clients arrive and judge hears various issues.

12:15 p.m.: Meet opposing counsel for plea bargain agreement for drug possession case.

1:00 p.m.: Quick lunch at desk, looking over emails and phone calls. Wait for witness to show up at 2:00.

2:00 p.m.: Witness doesn't show. Work on research for motion on attempted murder case involving Fourth Amendment right of seizure.

3:00 p.m.: Brief interview with police officers on felony assault case.

3:30 p.m.: Witness for 2:00 finally shows up with father and sister. Conduct fact-finding issue on domestic violence case. Witness recants some testimony and father pressures her not to testify against her husband, leaving ADA uncertain as to strength of case.

4:45 p.m.: Contact court clerks regarding hearing status of various cases.

5:10 p.m.: Review documents for money laundering and call witnesses and corporate officers for interviews in the next few days.

6:15 p.m.: Head home.

Federal prosecutor

Each federal district in the United States has a U.S. attorney, appointed by the president to serve a four-year term. Assistant U.S. attorneys are hired, not appointed, and therefore not affected when a new U.S. attorney is appointed. The Office of the U.S. Attorney, as a division of the Department of Justice, handles both civil and criminal litigation.

For the most part, federal prosecutors are concerned with violations of the United States Criminal Code, which includes crimes such as racketeering, wire fraud, civil rights violations, drug trafficking, securities violations, corruption by public officials, interstate fraud and certain types of robberies. Some crimes otherwise prosecuted under state law fall under the federal prosecutor's jurisdiction if they are interstate (like child kidnapping) or if they take place on federal property (an assault in a veteran's hospital, for example). The federal prosecutor may work with state prosecutors in order bring a particular offender to justice. Alternatively, a federal prosecutor may have state charges dropped in order for a defendant to be brought in front of a federal court. Sometimes the aims of the federal and state prosecutor conflict and the politics of the different departments can decide fate of the accused.

A federal prosecutor prepares for trial much like a county prosecutor does, working with law enforcement personnel like the FBI, the sheriff's office and local state officials. In addition to meeting with witnesses, gathering and presenting the evidence, and building a persuasive case, federal prosecutors work extensively with prosecutors in other jurisdictions. The federal prosecutor is bound by the federal rules of procedure in court and, because the federal sentencing guidelines are extremely stringent, often has very little say in sentencing.

Many lawyers become federal prosecutors in order to facilitate large-scale change in their district. Because the job of a federal prosecutor can be very high-profile, it can also lead to public office, as it did for Rudolph Giuliani who, before serving as mayor of New York, was the U.S. Attorney in Manhattan responsible for the conviction of many notorious organized crime and white-collar crime figures. Some federal prosecutors move into private practice or are elected to a judgeship.

In order to become a federal prosecutor, you must have at least two years legal – and usually litigation – experience. Federal prosecutors often have a considerable amount of legal experience before joining the U.S. attorney's office. A significant and prominent interest in public service is also important and one of the things that prosecutors' offices look for. "You need to be willing to uphold the law, even if it means ignoring your personal feelings about whether the law is right," says one fourth-year federal prosecutor. The U.S. attorney's office also requires stringent background checks, multiple interviews, drug testing and, in some districts, even polygraph examinations. The U.S. attorney's office requires a commitment to the department for three years.

A U.S. attorney in the Eastern District of New York makes a starting salary of $70,000. Most districts pay less and some salaries start as low as $45,000. Advancement is based on experience and performance, and pay raises are usually fixed. As you continue to work in the prosecutor's office, you may be assigned to a particular division or task force (organized crime, for example). The federal prosecutor can work quite reasonable hours or around the clock when she is going to trial. The stakes are very high in federal prosecutions, and the sentences are usually higher than at the state level. While the work can be exciting, it can also be extremely stressful. Like their state counterparts, federal prosecutors face the ethical dilemmas inherent in our criminal justice system. "I wish it was black and white," says one first-year U.S attorney. "It's not. Most of the time I know I'm putting the bad guys away, but sometimes there's some doubt. And that can keep you up at night."

Public defender

The public defender might be the unsung hero of the legal system. As a government employee, he makes relatively little for a litigator. He has little say over his cases and often works with the defendants that no one else wants. He doesn't have the resources that the district attorney's office has and must often engage in his own investigations. Many of his cases seem almost hopeless and, to the victims of crime, he appears almost as bad as his defendants. So why does he do this job?

For one thing, public defenders are integral to the criminal justice system. The law affords everyone the right to an attorney including those who cannot afford one. "It's a mistake to say that we're against the system. We're part of the system," observes one public defender. Public defenders work for government agencies or are private lawyers paid an hourly rate by the state. Either way, there's not a lot of money to be made.

There are public defenders at the state, federal and appellate levels. At the state level, a public defender represents impoverished clients in state criminal court, handling everything from small violations to juvenile offenses to violent crime cases. She is responsible for acquiring all background information on the case, interviewing witnesses and filing the appropriate papers and motions in court, as well as preparing for trial and negotiating plea bargains. Although previous litigation experience is always looked upon as an asset, a lawyer can become a state public defender in his first year after law school.

The public defender at the federal level represents those who cannot afford private representation in federal court. An assistant federal public defender does both trial and appellate work in the U.S. district courts and the circuit courts of appeal. In general, a candidate for the federal public defender's office must already have a few years of serious litigation experience, preferably in criminal court.

Some states have a separate agency for public defenders working at an appellate level. These appellate defenders work with appeals either in state or federal court, preparing for appellate-level hearings or representing defendants at the post-conviction level. Their job is to make sure that the defendant has had a fair and impartial trial and that his treatment in the justice system continues to be appropriate and fair. Some appellate defenders specialize in capital cases (cases involving the death penalty).

First-year public defenders will find themselves in court very quickly, defending petty thieves and vandals and the like. They might work odd shifts and have only a few minutes to meet with each client before appearing before a judge. Often, the defense attorney's job will be to get a fair plea bargain for his client. Public defenders spend a good portion of every day either in court for hearings or in jails with their clients. Gradually, as the public defender increases in skill and knowledge of the legal system, he will start trying more complicated misdemeanors and eventually felonies. Most public defender agencies offer some kind of training, but most of a public defender's duties are learned on the job and on his feet.

Like their adversaries across the aisle, public defenders get court experience and criminal law experience very quickly. As a public defender, you will be representing clients in trials long before your friends with civil litigation jobs and, in some cases, before your classmates who became assistant district attorneys. As the defenders of the indigent and needy, public defenders can find immense satisfaction in helping someone who would otherwise be lost in the currents of the legal system. There will always be work for public defenders, and the litigation experience is unparalleled.

Being a public defender is, however, often an uphill battle. In many cases, the prosecution has a mountain of damning evidence and a defense attorney might start to feel as if his job is merely defending "guilty people." A public defender at an agency has very little say in which cases he takes and, while he may happily take on a burglary case, defending an alleged rapist can be a sobering experience. (A public defender can sometimes turn down a case, but this is rare and usually frowned upon.) The role of a criminal defense attorney is very demanding in any case, but the public defender often works with those considered "the dregs" of society and may have to face the victim or the victim's family in court every day.

Many public defenders enjoy the legal challenge. "I think my job is very creative," says one public defender. "I'm given a set of facts and the ADA's theory, and it's my job to see other perspectives. It's challenging." Others are devoted to making sure that even the most despised and vulnerable members of society are represented fairly. Some defenders see their role as ensuring that the prosecution is forced to put together the best prosecution it can, given that a person's freedom is at stake. Others have political or sociological views that clash with the established judicial or prison system. "I think you need a pretty strong belief system to do this job," says one public defender. "Not always – I mean, there are people who do it just for the experience. But it can wear you down, and it helps to really feel that you're contributing something."

Whatever their motivation, the ranks of public defenders are full of excellent lawyers. The salary at a state agency is generally commensurate with that at the district attorney's office, although in some jurisdictions a public defender can make much less. Salaries in the $40,000 range are common in big cities, although lawyers with more litigation experience enjoy a higher starting salary. Appellate defenders at the state level will make about as much as their trial counterparts. Federal public defenders make salaries similar to those of the U.S. attorneys in their area. This can be as much as a $70,000 starting salary in New York or as low as $45,000 elsewhere. Generally, a prospective public defender at any level will pass through a series of interviews and be asked to make a commitment of a certain number of years to the agency. (Three is a common number.) Most agencies look for evidence of interest in community service and helping the needy, from a legal or other standpoint.

Public defenders who are not part of an agency are assigned their cases by a court and paid by the hour. This hourly rate varies from jurisdiction to jurisdiction, but $25 to $40 an hour is a common range. Lawyers in every state have complained that the hourly rate set by courts chases many good would-be public defenders into different fields of law. Clearly, lawyers remain public defenders for reasons other than the money.

Public defenders can work many long hours, especially if they're on trial. However, the hours of a public defender, like those of an assistant district attorney, are not as unrelentingly demanding as those of corporate litigators. And while hiring is dependent on government budgets, the high turnover rate of public defenders means that new, eager lawyers are always wanted.

A Day in the Life of a Public Defender

8:30 a.m.: Arrive at office. Prepare for court.

9:00 a.m.: Appear in court for various arraignments, including robbery, assault, attempted murder, drunk and disorderly cases. Multiple arraignments for drug possession cases, both misdemeanor and felony.

12:30 p.m.: Break for lunch.

1:00 p.m.: Preliminary hearing for a felony drug possession case.

2:00 p.m.: Contact mental health professionals and schedule mental health intake for defendant charged with assault.

3:00 p.m.: Arrive at jail to speak with clients.

4:30 p.m.: Research and write motion for court on "intent to distribute" ketamine. Motion is due next week. Spend time on computer looking up statute and implications.

6:00 p.m.: Go home.

Private defense attorney

Private criminal lawyers do much of the same work as public defenders. They gather evidence, interview witnesses, prepare for trial, draft motions and other court papers, represent their clients in plea bargains and in preliminary hearings and guide their clients through the court system. However, since they do not work for government agencies, they have different salary opportunities and lifestyles. "Working for a firm, I have some input into the kinds of cases we take," says one litigator at a small criminal defense firm.

A private criminal lawyer may work in a large or small firm or as a solo practitioner. In general, a criminal lawyer in a law firm will have some area of specialty – felony cases, for example, or white-collar crime. As the years progress, the criminal lawyer can get very specialized indeed and become known for her representation of corporate clients charged with fraud or rapists or even serial killers. A solo practitioner may also specialize, depending on her resources. Like her counterpart in civil litigation, a solo practitioner will often handle a variety of criminal matters in the beginning of her career in order to establish herself.

Most law school graduates do not become private criminal attorneys in their first year out of law school. Law firms generally look for litigation experience, preferably at the criminal level. They want to hire someone who can bring something to the firm – either knowledge of the criminal court system, experience with particular defendants or a steady source of clients – and a private firm or solo practitioner can be choosier about its cases than a public defender. "A prosecutor's office or a public defender job will train you," says one private criminal attorney. "I think by the time you're working here, you need to have some solid trial experience. We don't do that many misdemeanors or violations, so there's not as much to train first-years with."

Firms therefore prefer to hire attorneys who already have the skills and experience to defend their clients. It doesn't really matter that the attorney may have previously been a prosecutor; most firms just want some criminal litigation experience and are not too concerned about which side a lawyer used to represent. It is not uncommon for former prosecutors to switch to defense practice or for defense attorneys to join the U.S. attorney's office. A large percentage of private criminal attorneys, either at firms or working as solo practitioners, have years of prior experience as state or federal prosecutors or defenders. Johnnie Cochran, the lead attorney in the criminal defense of O.J. Simpson, used to work for the Los Angeles District Attorney's Office as a prosecutor.

Most criminal defense firms are smaller than their corporate counterparts. A firm of 60 lawyers in three offices is considered a large criminal defense firm, while the attorneys at corporate firms can number in the hundreds. Criminal firms generally have smaller starting salaries. A starting salary of $40,000 or less is not unheard of; on the other hand, an attorney with five years experience could be making double or triple that amount. "I chose this job because I can still do trial law, which I love, while making a decent living," says one criminal defense lawyer. "It's not glamorous, but it's a lot better than the DAs office." All private attorneys – civil and criminal alike – have to think about billable hours and can put in extremely long hours at the office. At a more senior level, criminal defense attorneys are expected to bring in cases for their firm. Success in the firm is dependent on many things, but largely on how many cases you win.

Solo practitioners in the criminal field are subject to the same constraints and responsibilities as civil lawyers who have their own practice, in terms of paying staff, rent and keeping a small business afloat. Unlike their civil counterparts, however, they cannot usually count on repeat business from the same clients.

Other Public and Private Service Litigators

Government agencies

In addition to criminal prosecutors and defense lawyers, there are myriad other opportunities for litigators interested in working for the government. Virtually all federal agencies, from the Internal Revenue Service to the U.S. Patent and Trademark Office, have their own attorneys and, sometimes, their own litigators. The Securities and Exchange Commission has its own prosecutors to litigate violations of federal securities law. These attorneys are often former securities litigators from private firms. They enforce SEC regulations and conduct investigations into insider trading or possible fraud in the stock market. The IRS has its own fleet of litigators who investigate and prosecute cases of tax fraud on the part of corporate and individual taxpayers.

The military branch has its own laws and its own litigators, who serve in the Judge Advocate General's Corps (JAG Corps). Judge advocates are members of the armed forces whose primary function is to ensure that all members of the military adhere to the Uniform Code of Military Justice. The military not only has its own litigators but its own courts, with their own jurisdiction and procedural rules. Judge advocates usually get litigation experience very early in their careers and may work as prosecutors or for the defense in criminal trials and practice in military, state and federal courts. They prepare investigations and conduct trials like any other litigator, but they often have a host of other legal responsibilities as well, like advising officers and providing general legal services to the members of the military.

Military attorneys must make a four-year commitment to the sector of the armed forces for which they work, attend training sessions in military law and, in some cases, be prepared for combat. JAG lawyers could find themselves practicing law on a ship or overseas. Some attorneys enter the JAG Corps after law school, while others enroll in the training program during law school, in which case the military pays for most of their legal education. The salary for JAG lawyers ranges from $45,000 to $58,000 over the course of the four years. The military also pays for housing and various cost-of-living expenses.

Some states have a civil legal aid division which helps indigent people with housing complaints, matrimonial law and children's issues. These lawyers represent clients in different state courts like family court, juvenile court or housing court. It's quite possible to start work as a litigator in a public service agency right out of law school. These agencies have limited funding and are always looking for eager young litigators. As might be expected, these agencies pay very little, often as little as $25,000 in some states. The work, however, can be extremely rewarding. Other government jobs require more experience. SEC prosecutors generally have at least a few years of litigation experience, usually in securities litigation. Similarly, IRS attorneys have prior experience as tax attorneys. Such positions tend to pay more than entry-level jobs, with SEC prosecutors usually earning upwards of $50,000.

Most government attorneys work standard business hours, although exceptions are made during trials and other hectic periods. Government jobs also offer substantial medical and dental benefits and vacations. "I never wanted to try the firm life," says one government litigator. "It pays well, but they really work you over. Here, I work hard, but I have more control over my life." One downside is dealing with the bureaucracy of often inefficient government programs.

Nonprofit organizations

The Southern Poverty Law Center, the National Association for the Advancement of Colored People and the ACLU are all non-governmental legal organizations that provide services to the community. They and many other private or not-for-profit organizations offer opportunities for litigators. The salaries are probably not high and you have to be relatively comfortable with each organization's legal agenda, but for committed attorneys, private service agencies provide valuable opportunities both to gain litigation experience and to fight for change in society.

These groups generally have limited funding and seek lawyers who already have litigation experience and a proven track record of community service. The work hours can be very long or quite reasonable, depending on your level of commitment. Competition for these jobs can be quite fierce. Benefits and salaries depend on the individual's funding, but most starting salaries are quite poor, as low as $22,000. "Obviously, you don't join the ACLU for the money," observes an ACLU litigator. "You join – at least I joined – because you want to make some real changes in the world around you."

Corporations

Many corporations have their own in-house counsel. These attorneys frequently come from litigation departments at large law firms. As in-house lawyers, they might work on pending litigations, but their current responsibilities are more likely to involve offering advice or drafting policies in order to prevent litigation. Most corporations will do anything to avoid ending up in court. These former litigators therefore actually do very little litigation. "Most of my job is avoiding litigation," says one attorney who works in-house at publishing company. "It's a lot of drafting contracts and things like that. If I do my job, we shouldn't be anywhere near a courtroom."

In order to become an in-house counsel, you must generally have over three years experience in litigation at a law firm. The larger and more complex the corporation, the more qualifications necessary for the job. Smaller companies don't usually have in-house counsel, but if they do, they don't require as much experience. Salaries for in-house lawyers are usually lower than those of large-firm litigators, but a first-year salary of $100,000 is not unheard of. It depends on the corporation, the attorney's experience and the duties she is expected to perform. The hours will likely be more reasonable than a big-firm attorney and the benefits are excellent.

The Role of the Junior Litigator

CHAPTER 11

Legal Documents

With all the references to legal writing and court papers, you might be wondering what kind of documents litigation associates work on. The answer varies from firm to firm, but, generally, first-year associates work on either pre-trial motions or internal memoranda for research issues.

Pre-trial papers include discovery motions, motions to dismiss, subpoenas, orders to show cause and myriad other documents. A motion might be made to the court to request dismissal of a cause of action, to ask for a ruling on a specific legal issue or to determine what evidence will and will not be allowed into trial. A first-year associate will often work on one small aspect of a motion – one research issue, for example. It may result in just one paragraph in the motion papers, but researching the issue might take days.

There are a host of other papers that need to be prepared for litigation. Some are as simple as filling out a form; others might be lengthy briefs arguing a particular issue of law. As a junior associate in a large firm, you will probably only be responsible for part of a pre-trial motion or brief. If you work at a smaller firm (with fewer lawyers assigned to a case), then you will probably get more responsibility, sooner. You might draft affidavits for witnesses, prepare interrogatories, or research and write an entire memorandum of law in support of a motion for summary judgment.

A junior associate will likely prepare internal memoranda for a partner or senior associate. The partner might have an idea for an argument but not be sure how strong it is. Or she might want to know more about the history of a particular law. While these research memos can take just as long (and be just as important) as papers submitted to court, they will only be seen internally by others at the firm.

In the courtroom: Stages in a typical civil lawsuit

The following sections lay out the stages of typical civil and criminal proceedings and the part that junior litigators play in them.

The dispute

Typically, there are two or more parties involved in a dispute. (For simplicity's sake, we will assume there are two parties involved in the suit). When it becomes clear that they cannot settle their differences amicably, they hire attorneys. Usually, it is the senior partner at a firm who officially takes the case.

Both sides will informally discuss the demands made by one party and determine what demands, if any, are reasonable under current law. While it will be the senior attorney – usually a partner – who makes most of the decisions, associates at varying levels may be doing research. Often, letters are exchanged between the two parties' attorneys. (Formal letters are required to start a lawsuit in some states, but the defendant's attorneys are not required to answer them). The complaining party's attorneys identify what exactly their client wants and how her claim is supported by law. The opposing attorneys formulate a legal defense to the demands. The attorneys for both sides may meet to see if an amicable conclusion can be reached; such meetings typically are attended by the partner and/or senior associates.

The pleadings

The plaintiff, the party bringing the suit, will file papers in court to start the action. These papers usually include a formal complaint, a copy of which she will also "serve" on (deliver to) the defendant. The complaint will identify the defendant, the basis for her claim against him and the relief she is requesting from the court. (For certain kinds of lawsuits, the initial pleading is called a petition and the complainant is known as the petitioner instead of the plaintiff.) Usually, associates will actually draft the complaint. Junior associates will engage in research while senior associates will do the drafting and begin to interview witnesses. Preliminary work on discovery will begin – both sides will begin to draft motions to demand files and other materials from the opposing party.

After the complaint is filed, the defendant will have a certain amount of time to respond with an answer, in which he will either admit or deny the plaintiff's allegations and lay out the grounds for his defense. Again, the division of labor on this pleading is similar to that for the complaint, with junior associates working on the research, senior associates doing the drafting and partners overseeing the process.

Discovery

Pre-trial discovery can be the longest part of a civil suit, taking anywhere from a few weeks to several years. Both sides begin to interview witnesses and draft motions to request files, physical evidence and access to certain people. Common discovery tools include written interrogatories, oral depositions and subpoenas requesting witnesses to appear or produce documents. Office space is cleared to make room for files requested from the other party, and junior associates begin a document review. Associates also draft discovery motions, with the partner supervising and making sure no stone is unturned. If both sides are making discovery motions, then both sides also have to engage in document production as well as document review.

Research and motion practice

Whether it's a disagreement over a discovery issue or a pre-trial question of another sort, this is the time where both sides start filing motions with the court. The defendant's attorney will file motions to limit issues, to dismiss claims or to compel the plaintiffs to do something. The plaintiff's attorneys will respond to these motions and draft some of their own. Typically, a senior or mid-level associate will write a motion and ask junior associate to do research and minor drafting on specific issues. Motion papers can include witness affidavits, memoranda of law (sometimes called "points and authorities") and documentary evidence. The partner will decide ultimately what issues are worth fighting for and what avenues to pursue. This stage of the civil lawsuit can take anywhere from a few weeks to a few years.

Trial preparation

Before every trial, a pre-trial conference is scheduled, at which the judge will rule on certain motions and parties will meet. Generally, partners will be heavily involved at this stage, as issues get clarified and the judge's decisions impact the future of the case. Most cases are settled at or by this time. Between the discovery, motion practice and conferences, associates are usually frantic.

Jury selection

If it seems that a settlement is unlikely, the firm will intensify its pre-trial preparations. This includes creating exhibits (usually done by associates), preparing witnesses (usually handled by senior associates and partners), writing arguments (the task of both partners and senior associates) and choosing a jury. The attorneys on both sides will engage in voir dire, a formal questioning of prospective jury members from a jury pool. Choosing the right jury is vitally important to the case, and a partner will probably do the voir dire himself. (At the very least, it will be a senior associate.) A settlement is still possible at this stage.

The trial

Trials can last anywhere from a few days to a few months. The trial might take place in a different city, depending on which state and which court has jurisdiction over the case. The partner and associates will be in court virtually every day. The partner or a senior associate will be speaking in court, questioning witnesses and presenting evidence. Junior associates will be responsible for making sure that the partner has everything she needs and getting last-minute information during the trial.

The judgment

At the conclusion of the evidence, each side will give a closing argument and the judge will issue instructions to the jury. Normally, the standard of proof in a civil case is a preponderance of the evidence, meaning that in order to find the defendant liable the jury must find it more likely than not that the defendant is responsible for the injuries alleged by the plaintiff. The jury will return with a judgment or verdict in favor of either the defendant or the plaintiff. If the jury finds the defendant liable, it will also decide the amount of damages (if any) to award the plaintiff. Then the judge will dismiss the jury.

Post-trial practice

Parties may file post-trial motions to convince the judge that there has been a mistake or that a different verdict should be entered. Plaintiffs who did not get what they were asking for may seek a different form of relief. In many cases, the losing party will choose to appeal the decision in a higher court. If so, different lawyers may be hired for the appellate process. If the plaintiff has won, she will seek to collect the judgment at soon as possible, and both sides will discuss the methods of collecting the damages.

In the courtroom: Stages in a typical criminal action

The crime

Usually only the prosecutor is involved at this stage. As the police conduct the investigation, the prosecutor will advise them whether he has enough evidence to file charges. A junior prosecutor will discuss the case with his supervisors who will advise him what crime to charge the offender with. After a formal charge has been filed, usually in the form of a complaint, the prosecutor might go to a judge to obtain an arrest warrant.

The arrest and arraignment

As the offender goes through the criminal justice system, he will either be assigned a defense attorney or hire one of his own. Junior defense attorneys will gather information pertinent to the case, make witness lists and request discovery. Prosecutors will make decisions about the charges, based on information provided by the police.

After arrest, the offender is booked at the police precinct and appears before the judge at an arraignment, his first hearing in court. He pleads not guilty or guilty and usually pays bail (if offered) or remains in jail (for more serious offenses or if he cannot meet the bail requirement). If the charge is a misdemeanor, then he may have the opportunity to pay his fine and go home. He might be required to be present at a second hearing to discuss bail. The defense attorney might know her client from well before the arrest or she may be meeting him for the first time at his arraignment.

Gathering evidence

If the prosecutor's office has decided to pursue the case (usually a decision of a high-ranking prosecutor), then the junior prosecutors work with the police to issue warrants for searches and continue to gather information against the defendant. The defense attorney will work with her client and interview witnesses. She may even hire her own investigators to do research, chase down witnesses and examine the crime scene. At this stage, prosecutors and defense attorneys may meet to discuss a plea bargain. Most cases end here; some go on to trial. (The vast majority of cases end in a guilty plea before trial.) For more serious crimes, the prosecutors will prepare for a grand jury in order to obtain an indictment.

The grand jury

A grand jury, normally made up of 16 to 23 citizens, decides whether the prosecutor has enough information to charge the defendant with committing a crime. The process may take days or weeks and, unlike the jurors at trial, the grand jury members can question the witnesses themselves. The prosecutor will present his witnesses and evidence and usually junior prosecutors will be heavily involved at this stage. If the crime is very serious, a senior prosecutor may speak to the grand jury, while junior prosecutors help prepare the evidence and question minor witnesses. In some states, a defendant may waive his right to an indictment by a grand jury. This is common when the defendant has agreed to a plea bargain.

Trial preparation and motion practice

If the grand jury votes to indict, the case is set for a trial date and a judge is assigned. Both sides continue to gather evidence to shape their cases. Any preliminary examinations necessary (by psychiatrists, for example) will be scheduled at this point.

As in civil cases, both sides will engage in motion practice and limited pre-trial discovery proceedings. Junior attorneys will do the research and write the motion papers. Senior prosecutors will oversee the case and often make decisions about what motions to file and why. The prosecutors will continue to interview witnesses, gather information and review documents. Plea bargain talks may continue as more evidence is unearthed. As the court rules on the motions, the nature of the case may change significantly.

The jury

The criminal defendant is entitled to trial by jury. The prosecution and defense will begin the process of choosing and questioning a jury, known as voir dire. This process will probably involve senior attorneys on both sides, as the right jury can make or break a case. Each side has a number of peremptory challenges which they can use to eliminate a potential jury member. The ideal jury is free from prejudice and knows nothing about the case, but attorneys may be vitally interested in the background of each jury member. Junior attorneys on both sides will prepare questions for the jury.

The trial

A trial may take days or weeks, perhaps months. Criminal trials tend to be much shorter than their civil counterparts. The lead prosecutor on the case and the most senior defense attorney will be responsible for the big-picture decisions and will communicate most often with the judge. Junior attorneys will be in charge of preparing the evidence and less important witnesses. Senior attorneys will give the opening and closing arguments. Junior attorneys may be allowed to question less important witnesses, but their primary responsibility will be making sure that the attorneys in court have everything they need. Some cases only have one attorney on each side, in which case, they – and some support staff – will be responsible for everything occurring in trial!

The verdict

The judge will give the jury instructions on how to evaluate the charges. The burden is on the prosecution to prove the defendant's guilt beyond a reasonable doubt. The jury will deliberate for a set amount of time and return with a decision of guilty or not guilty. If found guilty, the defendant is taken into custody. Defense attorneys now have two things to prepare for: the sentencing hearing and, possibly, an appeal. Prosecution attorneys prepare their sentencing recommendations, based on information about the defendant's background, prior convictions and the seriousness of the crime.

There will be some kind of presentence report put together by the court's probation office, and the prosecution will prepare any witnesses for the hearing. The defense will also prepare to ask leniency for his client. Junior attorneys research relevant issues and help draft the sentencing report.

Sentencing

The judge will make a decision based on the presentence report, witness testimony at the hearing and the defendant's own words. At the hearing, the prosecution presents evidence for its sentence recommendation, using testimony from witnesses and experts and other material. Senior attorneys may not be as involved at this stage, although they will oversee the process. The defense presents challenges to the prosecution's findings and to the report. Both the victim and the defendant have a right to speak. Finally, after reviewing all the evidence, the judge will determine a sentence within statutory constraints, which can include time in prison, restitution to the victim or a fine to be paid to the government.

Post-conviction remedies

A losing defendant may file an appeal. The prosecution cannot appeal a verdict of not guilty, but it sometimes can appeal the sentence. The defendant might hire different defense attorneys who are better versed in the appeals process or have an appellate public defender assigned to the case. Senior attorneys usually handle appeals, but a junior attorney may be involved in legal research and may help draft the appellate brief. The defense counsel may re-interview people associated with the trial in order to familiarize herself with the case, but no witnesses will be allowed to testify in appellate court. The court might hear oral arguments from both sides in addition to reviewing written briefs and the record on appeal. If the appellate court decides to overturn the decision, both sides may prepare for a retrial, although the prosecution might decide not to try the case again.

Success on the Job

Everyone's experience as a litigator will be different. Whether you work at a large multinational law firm or in the office of a solo practitioner, with a public interest agency or at the U.S. attorney's office, your life will probably be quite intense. You will work long hours, have responsibility for one or more cases and other people will depend on you. The first few years of practice are often the hardest. As you gain experience and begin to work more efficiently, then your life might become easier. "The first year is where you have to prove yourself," observes one third-year attorney at a large firm.

For those who work at law firms, especially, the work might seem never-ending, with partners making unreasonable demands and your social life becoming a thing of the past. You "have to make an effort to keep your life going," says one junior litigator at a large firm. "It's really hard in the beginning, and you'll be asked to cancel your plans more than once." Meanwhile, at government jobs you'll be arguing with bored, unhelpful and frequently underpaid employees, meeting with clients who don't want to cooperate and struggling without the basic necessities of a legal career — like working pens, for example. You won't be paid much for your work either.

Minorities and women often feel extra pressure in large law firms. "The big firms are changing, but a majority of partners are still older, white men," says one female minority associate. "They can be pretty behind the times on a lot of issues." When it comes to change, it looks like firms are more receptive to women's issues than to minority concerns. Most firms, despite their initial hiring process, retain few minorities as senior associates and even fewer as partners, while virtually every major firm has at least a few prominent female partners. Both minorities and women sometimes complain that they have few mentors who really understand what they are going through. "I've been mistaken for a member of the support staff more than once," says one minority associate. "I don't think it has to do with the way I dress."

Many firms are attempting to address these issues. "I know at this firm, we're always making an effort to diversify our first-year class and be sensitive to minority issues," says one partner. "It's not always easy to change the way things are done, but a lot of the younger partners are bringing change."

If you can keep in mind some of the following suggestions, it might help your legal career move forward more smoothly.

- **Your first job doesn't have to be your last.** "Virtually everyone changes jobs in the legal profession," notes one senior associate. If you don't like what you're doing now but it's preparing you for a better job down the road, then maybe it's worthwhile to stick with it for a little longer.

- **Improve your current situation.** If there's a partner you'd like to work with (or a partner you really can't work with), see what you can do to make some changes. Talk to your mentor or another senior attorney. Identifying your likes and dislikes, as well as making the improvements you can, is a good start to getting more job satisfaction.

- **Keep your options open.** Attend continuing legal education courses and mingle with your fellow attorneys. Another interesting opportunity might show up where you least expect it — either within the same firm or elsewhere.

- **Don't give up on your social life.** Continue to devote time to the people and the hobbies you enjoy. Just because your plans get cancelled occasionally doesn't mean you have to throw in the towel.

- **Communicate.** Both firms and agencies will provide you with mentors. If things are getting rough, make sure you have someone to talk to, someone who can see things from a different perspective. You might get some good advice; and, at the very least, the mere act of talking might help.

- **Know your limits.** Don't work until you burn out. If you haven't been home before midnight for a while and there doesn't seem to be an end in sight, talk to someone. It can be really easy to get wrapped up in the work and forget everything else — you don't want to completely break down!

- **Recognize your job's limits.** If you are looking for something that this litigation job simply won't provide, now or ever, then you're resigning yourself to an unhappy existence for no reason. People become litigators for a variety of reasons. If you're starting to realize that your priorities are changing but your job won't, then you need to think about whether this is the best place for you.

Changing Jobs

Almost every lawyer changes jobs at least once. From large firm to small firm, from law firm to government agency, from agency to corporate counsel, lawyers move frequently from one position to another. Your goals as a litigator may change as you continue your career, and few lawyers stay in their first job forever.

If you are considering a change of employment at any level, you'll probably be working with a headhunter. Recruiters don't offer the only way to get lateral positions, but it is the most common, especially with law firms. Other methods include responding to ads in legal newspapers and networking. A legal headhunter or recruiter often specializes in a particular kind of job search — for example, lateral hiring or non-legal positions. A headhunter will often have established connections in various firms, because she has successfully placed people there before. This personal connection can speed your resume through the application process and bring it to the attention of someone who might be otherwise too distracted to read it.

Legal recruiters work for the law firm, not for you. Although they may be quite eager to place a good candidate with the right firm, they are hired, and paid, by the firm. They are therefore more interested in making the firm happy than in pleasing you. Many headhunters will want you to work with them exclusively. They'll give you a lot of reasons, but the basic fact is they don't want to spend a lot of time on a candidate who's already sending out a hundred resumes through dozens of other recruiters. Whether you decide to work with one headhunter or not is up to you, but make sure that no one sends out your resume without telling you first.

Keep in touch with your recruiters. They will be screening many candidates and you can get lost in the shuffle. Don't drive them crazy, but make sure they know that you're still actively looking. Try to meet with the headhunter in person at least once. It will help her put a face to the name and get to know you. And don't be persuaded to do things that you think are wrong. Don't get talked into interviewing for a firm that's just like the one you're trying to get away from! A headhunter should have a plan of action specific to you. Admittedly, his first loyalty is to the firms that hire him, but if a recruiter doesn't see you as a real person with unique skills or you just don't connect with him, then it's better that you find someone else to work with.

To find a good recruiter, you can ask friends at other firms or laterals at your own firm, or even talk to your firm's recruitment coordinator (but be discreet!). In all probability, you will have some names already; recruiters like to keep track of first-year attorneys and make frequent cold calls.

Final Analysis

Litigation is a very demanding career, full of long hours and high-pressure situations. It can also be extremely rewarding, on financial, professional and personal levels. The most important thing to remember when starting your litigation career — or any legal career, for that matter — is that law is essentially a specialized service industry. Your first obligation is to your clients. You want to protect their rights and ensure that they understand enough of the legal system to feel comfortable with the proceeding. A litigator who forgets this is doing his clients a disservice and will probably encounter problems during his career. And he won't have the same satisfaction that a good lawyer gets from a grateful client.

As difficult as it may be to become a successful litigator, it is just as difficult for many litigators to remember that there's a world outside of their job. Law is the kind of career you can easily take home with you after the day is done, but the happiest lawyers are those who strive for a balance between work, family and play. To avoid burnout in your career, make sure that you are making time for the people and activities that are important to you. And if your first job out of law school isn't the right one for you, take heart — litigators can always move from one field to another and even find use for their skills outside the legal world. With the number of lawsuits filed daily in America, there will always be a need for good litigators of all kinds. Ultimately, your career will only be shaped by one person: you.

APPENDIX

Sample Legal Forms

Below are some examples of legal forms and documents commonly used in litigation proceedings. While these forms resemble real documents, please note that they do not refer to actual courts, cases, parties or docket numbers. These samples should not be relied on as accurate representations of any specific court's forms or statements of the law; they simply provide generic prototypes of the kinds of papers prepared by litigators. The format of actual court documents will vary from state to state, from court to court and even from judge to judge.

Sample Complaint

A complaint is the first step in any legal proceeding. A complaint sets out the plaintiff's cause(s) of action (for example, breach of contract, nuisance or employment discrimination), the basic factual allegations against the defendant that support the cause of action and the relief the plaintiff seeks.

The complaint below is for a divorce suit in the (imaginary) state of Jupiter. Jupiter's divorce laws would establish the basis for the claim and the state's rules of civil procedure would govern the mechanics of the pleading — including the information that must be provided and the manner and time in which it must be served on (delivered to) the opposing party and filed with the court.

SUPERIOR COURT OF THE STATE OF JUPITER
COUNTY OF PLUTO

MARY SMITH	CASE NO: 36-86523-DM
V.	JUDGE: THOMAS JONES
JOHN Q. SMITH	COMPLAINT FOR DIVORCE

Jeremy King
123 Attorney Plaza
Some City, JU 55555
Tel: 555-123-4567
Attorney for Plaintiff

Now comes the Plaintiff, Mary Smith, who, first being duly sworn, represents to this Court the following:

1.   That, prior to filing this Complaint for Divorce, the Plaintiff was a resident of the State of Jupiter for more than six months, and a resident of the County of Pluto for more than 10 days.

2.   That the Plaintiff lives in the City of Lights, in Pluto County, and that the Defendant, John Smith, lives in the City of Lights, in Pluto County, and that venue and jurisdiction are proper in this Court.

3.   That the parties were married on July 4th, 1996, in Garden City, Jupiter, and the parties lived together as husband and wife until on or about October 16th, 2003, when they separated, and further, that the name of the Plaintiff, immediately prior to the marriage, was Mary A. Donaldson.

4.   That, during the marriage, the parties had two children:

Jane Smith, dob 7/4/98 and

Michael Smith, dob 9/1/00

and further, that the parties adopted no other children, and that the Plaintiff is not now pregnant.

5.   That the parties accumulated property during the marriage, which needs to be divided by this Court, including:

      a.   The marital home, located at 444 Shady Lane, City of Lights, JU 55556.

      b.   Two automobiles, one titled to the Plaintiff, with loan, and the other titled to Defendant, with loan, and

      c.   Miscellaneous personal property and furniture and personal effects, which are likely to be divided between the parties prior to trial, and

6.   That there has been a breakdown in the marriage relationship to the extent that the objects of matrimony have been destroyed, and, further, there remains no reasonable likelihood that this marriage can be preserved.

7.   That the Plaintiff will be unable to maintain or defend this action for divorce without an award of attorney's fees from the Defendant, who is gainfully employed at ABC Corporation.

8.   That the Plaintiff is perfectly suited to be the primary physical custodial parent of the minor children of the parties, and both parties are perfectly suited to be awarded joint legal custody of the children, and that this Court should enter an Order of joint legal custody, with physical custody to the Plaintiff mother (both temporarily and permanently), and with reasonable visitation to the Defendant, John Q. Smith, with the attendant order of support for the minor children, directing the Defendant, John Q. Smith, to pay support for the children in an amount recommended by the Jupiter Child Support Guidelines, based upon the income of each party.

WHEREFORE, Plaintiff prays that this Honorable Court will:

1.   Enter an Order of temporary physical custody of the minor children in favor of the Plaintiff, with joint legal custody of the children, and

2.   Enter an Order of support of the children, in the manner provided by law, and

3.   Equitably divide the marital property of the parties, and

4.   Enter an Order directing that the Defendant pay a portion of the attorneys' fees of the Plaintiff, and

6.   Provide the Plaintiff with such other, and further, relief, as the Plaintiff may show herself entitled to same.

[signature]: Mary Smith

Sample Answer

After a complaint has been served and filed, the defendant has a certain amount of time to respond with an answer. Note that the answer doesn't necessarily explain the arguments behind the party's defense; it merely states which issues the defendant concedes, if any, and what his stance is on issues where the parties disagree. A lawyer preparing any plea must be familiar with the rules of civil procedure since an improperly filed answer or complaint can result in a case being thrown out of court in an early stage.

SUPERIOR COURT OF THE STATE OF JUPITER
COUNTY OF PLUTO

MARY SMITH

V.

JOHN Q. SMITH

CASE NO: 36-86523-DM

JUDGE: THOMAS JONES

ANSWER TO COMPLAINT

Jeremy King
123 Attorney Plaza
Some City, JU 55555
Tel: 555-123-4567
Attorney for Plaintiff

Jennifer Jones
8228 Main Street
City of Lights, JU 55556
Tel: 555-987-6543
Attorney for Defendant

Now comes the Defendant, John Q. Smith, who answers Plaintiff's Complaint for Divorce as follows:

1.   ADMITTED.

2.   ADMITTED.

3.   ADMITTED.

4.   ADMITTED.

5.   ADMITTED.

6.   NEITHER ADMITTED NOR DENIED, as the Defendant does not have sufficient knowledge to admit or deny this statement.

---

7.   DENIED, for the reason that the statement is untrue: The Plaintiff is gainfully employed, and/or owns a business, and Plaintiff has sufficient income to pay her own attorney's fees.

8.   ADMITTED IN PART, AND DENIED IN PART: The Defendant is just as qualified as the Plaintiff to be the primary physical custodian of the minor children of the parties.

Further, Defendant agrees that the provisions of the Jupiter Child Support Guidelines control the support to be paid between the parties, based upon the factors expressed therein.

WHEREFORE, the Defendant prays that this Honorable Court will:

1.   Equitably divide the property of the parties, and

2.   Provide for the minor children of the parties, in a joint physical custody arrangement, with support according to the Jupiter Child Support Guidelines, and

3.   Deny Plaintiff's request for attorneys fees, and

4.   Enter a Judgment of Divorce, and

5.   Provide the Defendant such other, and further, relief, as the Defendant may show himself entitled to same.

Further, Defendant prays not.

[signature]: John Q. Smith

Sample Opposition to Motion For Summary Judgment

A motion for summary judgment may be filed by either party who argues that, given the case the other side has presented so far, it is not necessary to proceed to trial — in effect, that the basic facts are not in dispute and that under those facts the moving party wins as a matter of law. In opposition to a summary judgment motion, a responding party will likely argue not only that the party making the motion is wrong in his interpretation of the law, but also that there are essential questions of fact that must be decided at trial before any legal conclusions can be reached. Unlike a pleading or affidavit, which may be prepared by an attorney but which present factual allegations of a party or witness, a memorandum of law (sometimes called a statement of points and authorities) is an attorney's document, his or her argument about the law.

Below is a portion of a legal memorandum submitted in support of a plaintiff's opposition to a summary judgment motion in a case involving alleged employment discrimination and defamation. Note that a statement of facts precedes the legal argument, in which the plaintiff refutes each of the defendant's arguments one by one.

**SUPERIOR COURT OF THE STATE OF JUPITER
COUNTY OF PLUTO**

RACHEL JONES,
    Plaintiff,

v.

XYZ CORPORATION, OSWALD APPLE,
ROCCO PEAR, JANET ORANGE inclusive,
    Defendants

                                           Case No. 12345

Sheila Litigator,
Attorney for Plaintiff
RACHEL JONES

          POINTS AND AUTHORITIES IN OPPOSITION TO
              MOTION FOR SUMMARY JUDGMENT

Date: 6/3/03
Time: 12:00 pm
Dept: 60
Disc. Cutoff: 7/3/03
Motion Cutoff: 6/4/03
Trial Date: _____

Plaintiff Rachel Jones opposes defendants' motion for summary judgment on the grounds that whether plaintiff was wrongfully demoted, whether defendants had a valid business reason for discriminating against her on the basis of her sex, and whether defendant Rocco Pear's defamation of her was privileged present triable issues of material fact.

FACTS

In 1994, defendant XYZ Corp., through its Director of the Department of Information and Development, defendant Rocco Pear, offered plaintiff a position as a supervisor in that Department. According to the written offer of a position, plaintiff would, among other duties, process and oversee the vacation and overtime requests for secretaries in that department. As a supervisor, she came within XYZ's supervisory and classified confidential staff employment policy.

Plaintiff worked in that capacity for six years. She was paid a salary of approximately $63,000 a year. She also received other benefits, including travel pay and an expense account. Her total compensation was about $85,000 a year.
Plaintiff received high marks for her performance as the Information and Development supervisor. She received few performance appraisals, but XYZ employees knew that an absence of evaluations reflected an absence of areas that needed critical improvement. Those evaluations she did receive were positive.

Plaintiff and defendant Rocco Pear nonetheless had substantial differences during this period. Defendant Pear was frequently intoxicated, at which times he groped at plaintiff, including by putting his hands on her breasts. After plaintiff complained in July 2000 to XYZ executive director Oswald Apple about defendant Rocco Pear's drinking, Rocco Pear cut back on the amount of work plaintiff was assigned. He also refused to support her exercise of her supervisorial authority over the secretaries in the department. At one point, plaintiff asked Jane Smith, one of those secretaries, to copy documents required for a meeting later that day. Smith refused first to take the documents to the photocopying department and then to pick them up. Defendant Rocco Pear refused to take any action to demonstrate plaintiff's authority to Ms. Smith or to any other secretary.

In August 2000, Information and Development became a higher-level department, and defendant Rocco Pear became a higher-level SFA associate executive director. Plaintiff retained her position as a supervisor but she was the only mid-level supervisor. On May 9, 2002, plaintiff again requested a promotion, which defendant Rocco Pear endorsed to Oswald Apple. Jones asked Janet Orange, manager of the Department of Human Resources Management, to review the request, and Orange recommended that the request be denied.

On September 24, 2002, plaintiff asked that her request be re-evaluated. Rocco Pear passed the request along to Oswald Apple, who stated that he could not consider the matter further until after the company's annual meeting. On December 3, 2002, Oswald Apple told plaintiff that he was turning down her request for a promotion because she was not performing supervisory duties.

Plaintiff responded to the news that she was not actually a supervisor by consulting attorney Mary White. On March 24, 2003, Ms. White wrote defendant Jones a demand letter in which she outlined causes of action for breach of contract, negligence, and retaliation. This letter caused defendant Rocco Pear to announce that he had had it with plaintiff, that he would not give her any more work, that he did not want to share office space with her, and that he was tired of plaintiff's gossiping about his womanizing and drinking. On April 5, 2002, Ms. White wrote XYZ president Martha Brown stating that defendant Pear's action constituted unlawful retaliation. XYZ's cabinet and board of directors live throughout the state of Jupiter; to ensure that each understood the organization's treatment of plaintiff, Ms. White sent a copy of the letter to each one at home.

Ms. White received their addresses from plaintiff, who provided her with a directory of the names. Nothing on the directory stated that the information was confidential. Plaintiff knew that XYZ had a policy preventing vendors and members from acquiring the names and addresses, but no one ever told her that XYZ had a policy against their disclosure to its employees or that a policy prohibited its employees from using the information.

Defendants nonetheless acted shocked. Although plaintiff only admitted providing the information to Ms. White, defendant Rocco Pear told Orange that she had admitted to stealing the information. On May 2, 2003, Orange issued a written reprimand to plaintiff. At the same time, another supervisory employee reported that plaintiff had told her about Rocco Pear's earlier sexual harassment of her. Although plaintiff insisted that she did not want to pursue the allegations of sexual harassment, XYZ'ss management said that she could not work under Mr. Rocco Pear while it investigated them.

Plaintiff was therefore transferred nominally to the Finance and Research Department. In actuality, she was given very little to do. Although she still goes to work each day and receives a salary, she spends most days doing nothing but making a rare photocopy. Although her salary has remained the same, she has lost her travel pay and expense account.

ARGUMENT

1. The standard for granting summary judgment

Summary judgment shall be granted if all the papers submitted show there is no triable issue of material fact and that the moving party is entitled to a judgment as a matter of law. Jup. Code Civ. Proc. §3457c(c). A defendant is entitled to summary judgment if the record establishes that none of the plaintiff's asserted causes of actions can prevail as a matter of law. Hunter vs. Ronald White Corporation (1985) 43 CAl.2d 1095, 1207. A defendant moving for summary judgment must conclusively negate a necessary element of the plaintiff's case and show there is no material issue of fact that requires a trial. Ibid.

The moving defendant has the burden of introducing evidence that the plaintiff's action is without merit on any legal theory. Gilbert vs. Park Towers Association (1992) 15 Cal.App.3rd 1041, 1064. Once the defendant has met that burden, the burden shifts to the plaintiff to show that a triable issue of material fact exists. Jup.Code Civ. Proc. §3457c(o)(1). But if the defendant fails to meet that burden, the adverse party has no burden to demonstrate the claim's validity, and the court must deny the motion. Huntert, supra, 15 Cal.App.3rd at 1064.

Instead of introducing evidence that would negate the plaintiff's action, a moving defendant may introduce the plaintiff's own factually devoid discovery responses to demonstrate that it has no case. Hurley vs. Lizard Prodution Associates, Inc. (1995) 34 Cal.App.4th 583, 589-593. The burden of proof would then be on the plaintiff to introduce evidence that would show a triable issue of material fact. Id., at 593. But the defendant does not meet its burden merely by asserting that the plaintiff has no evidence. Thurston vs. Third Howell Inc. (1973) 76 Cal.App.4th 175, 186. Instead, the defendant must submit discovery responses that would conclusively foreclose any cause of action. Id. at 186-187.

When no or insufficient affidavits or other evidence is submitted to demonstrate the absence of an issue of material fact, the court may treat the motion as in legal effect one for judgment on the pleadings. Glass Corporation vs. Ginger Gilligan (1993) 145 Cal.App.4th 556, 569. In that case, the motion performs the same function as a general demurrer. Ibid. A general demurrer will not test whether a complaint is ambiguous or uncertain or states essential facts only inferentially or conclusorily. Mary Anne Cosmetics v. Professor Kaplan Cookies (1987) 101 Cal.App.3d 146, 160. The defendants' failure to challenge those defects by way of special demurrer waives them. John Skipper v. Natalie Lovey Corp. (1971) 152 Cal.App.3d 977, 994.

2. The supervisory employee policy's arbitration clause does not require the employee to arbitrate.

When interpreting a contract calling for arbitration, the court should give effect to the parties' intentions, in light of the usual and ordinary meaning of the contractual language and the circumstances under which the agreement was made. John T. Wright vs. Flying Inc. (1983) 50 Cal.3d 738, 744. A form arbitration contract should be construed (cont'd)

Sample Interrogatory

An interrogatory is a form of pre-trial discovery in which one party requests that the other answer a list of questions regarding the subject of the lawsuit. In response to an interrogatory, the opposing party must provide either answers or legal reasons for not answering.

**UNITED STATES DISTRICT COURT
FOR THE DISTRICT OF SATURN**

UNITED STATES OF AMERICA,
Plaintiff,

CIVIL ACTION NO. 78-98032T

v.

GARDNER GREEN d/b/a
COMMON COURT APARTMENTS;

and KRISTIE BLACK,

Defendants.

UNITED STATES' FIRST SET OF
INTERROGATORIES TO DEFENDANT
GARDNER GREEN d/b/a
COMMON COURT APARTMENTS;

To: Gardner Green
P.O. Box 1234
Some City, JU 55555

Pursuant to Rule 33 of the Federal Rules of Civil Procedure, Plaintiff United States requests that Defendant Green answer, in writing and under oath, the following Interrogatories and that a copy of such answers be served upon the Plaintiff within thirty (30) days after the service of these Interrogatories. In the event that Defendant Green objects only to part of an interrogatory, he is required to furnish the information requested in the interrogatory that is not included within his partial objection.

DEFINITIONS

For the purposes of these interrogatories the following definitions are employed:

1.   "Documents" as used herein are defined as documents, records, books, papers, contracts, memoranda, invoices, correspondence, notes, photographs, drawings, charts, graphs, other writings, recording tapes, recording discs, mechanical or electronic information storage or recording elements (including any information stored on a computer), and any other "documents" as defined in Rule 34 of the Federal Rules of Civil Procedure. If a document has been prepared in several copies, or additional copies have been made that are not identical (or are no longer

identical by reason of subsequent notation or other modification of any kind whatever), each nonidentical copy is a separate document.

2.   "Identify," "identification," or "identity" have the following meanings:

a.   when used in reference to a natural person it means to state the person's full name, current residence and business addresses, current residence and business telephone numbers and, if applicable, their title, dates of employment, and job description. If their current addresses are unknown, provide the last known business and residence address;

b.   when used in reference to a document it means to state the type of document (e.g., letter, memorandum, telegram, chart, etc.), its author and originator, its date or dates, all addressees and recipients, and its present location or custodian. If any such document was but is no longer in your possession or subject to your control, state what disposition was made of it.

c.   when used in reference to a legal entity, the structure of the business (i.e., corporation, partnership, sole proprietorship, association), a brief description of the nature of the business, and the business address and telephone number;

d.   used in reference to real property, the full address, legal description of the property, the type of structure (e.g., commercial, single-family residential, multi-unit dwelling) and the number of units.

INTERROGATORIES

1.   Documents pertaining to ownership, financial, management or other proprietary interest or has had such an interest at any time since January 1, 1987.

2.   For each piece of real property listed in response to Interrogatory 4, please provide the following information:

a.   Nature of the interest and date each interest was acquired and, if applicable, relinquished;

b.   Name, address and type of interest of any other person(s), corporations, companies, associations or other legal entities besides defendant(s) having ownership, financial, management or other proprietary interest in property;

c.   If such property is residential rental property, state the number of dwelling units located on each property;

d.   If such property is residential rental property, state the name, last known address, last known telephone number, description of duties and date of service for each person (including defendant) engaged in any way in the rental of dwelling units at each property for the period March 1, 1988 to the present.

3.   Please state whether any apartment building owned or managed by Defendant Green has ever been the subject of a complaint, either oral or written, of any type of housing discrimination, either to Defendant Green, his representatives or agents, or to any state, local or federal agency such as the Department of Housing and Urban Development, a local military housing referral office, or a local fair housing agency. If so, state the name and address of every complainant, the date of the complaint, the details of the complaint, to whom it was made, the defendant or

representatives of the defendant who dealt in any way with the complaint, and the disposition of the matter. Identify all documents relating to such complaints.

4.   Identify the owner(s) of the residential rental property known as the "Common Court Apartments" located at 8783 Hyde Street, Dover, Arkansas 67208, and the legal form of ownership (i.e., whether there is sole ownership, or whether there is a corporation, a partnership or other legal entity which owns the property). (cont'd)

Sample Research Memorandum On A Legal Issue

This is an example of an in-house research memorandum on a legal issue. A supervising attorney identifies a legal issue that needs clarification or an argument that needs more support, and a junior attorney produces a memorandum much like this for internal use only. It is not to be served on opposing counsel or submitted to the judge; the argument, however, may be incorporated into a memorandum to be filed with the court.

LAWYERS, LITIGATORS AND ATTORNEYS, LLP

10 CENTER PLAZA

SOMEWHERE, NEPTUNE 12345

TO: Partner A

FROM: Associate B

RE: University's liability for injuries suffered by resident student's guest

FACTS

Client P. was staying in a dormitory at Pleasontan University as a resident student's guest. The semester had just ended and the dormitory was to be vacated three days later. Most of the students had already left. Client was in the dorm room alone at 2:30 a.m. The room's other occupants were visiting another student and were due back momentarily. Two unidentified men entered the room (which was unlocked); while one stood guard the other assaulted client and stole personal property.

The dormitory forms a quadrant with all room doors facing inward. It is impossible to see the room doors from any place other than the hallways. Security guards are supposed to patrol the halls, but the only place anyone had seen guards was in the parking lot looking for illegally parked cars and students drinking in their cars. The windows to the ground floor rooms can be easily pried open, and the room door locks are a simple pushbutton type that can be easily popped open with a student I.D. card. Also, some of the room keys fit more than one dorm room door. It is unknown if there is any official policy regarding guests spending the night, but they routinely do so and no one has ever been told it is against school policy.

ISSUE

Under what theory may the university be held liable for client's injuries?

SUMMARY

A college or university owes resident students the same duty to take reasonable steps to protect them from foreseeable criminal activity that a landlord owes a tenant or a condominium association owes a resident. It may also be held liable for misrepresenting a dormitory's safety or security. Client, being a guest, probably cannot show reliance on any misrepresentation. A good argument can be made, however, that the school owed her the same duty it owed to resident students.

DISCUSSION

1. School's duty as a landlord

In Crieghton v. State (N.Y.App. 1982) 476 N.Y.Supp.2d 729, a student at a state university was accosted in the laundry room of her dormitory, taken to a dorm room, and raped. Plaintiff sued the state for negligence and won. The court held that when the state acted in a proprietary capacity as a landlord it owed the resident students the same duty to take reasonable steps to protect them from foreseeable criminal activity that a private landlord owes a tenant. The evidence showed that strangers were not uncommon in the dorm hallways, that there had been numerous complaints about strangers loitering in the hallways and lounges, and that there had been numerous crimes in the dormitories, including armed robbery, burglaries, and one prior rape by a nonstudent. Despite having notice of the foregoing, and despite the fact that the dormitory outer doors had locking mechanisms, the doors were left unlocked at all hours. The court held that the failure to lock the outer doors was a breach of the state's duty as a landlord and a proximate cause of plaintiff's injuries.

In Jones v. State of California (Cal.App. 1980) 151 Cal.Rptr. 725 a mother whose daughter was raped and murdered in a state university dorm room brought a wrongful death action against the state. The trial court held that the facts alleged in the original complaint and in a proposed amended complaint showed that the student had a "landlord-tenant relationship-plus" with the university (id., at 735), and that an attack such as the one on the plaintiff's daughter was foreseeable because the university was aware of prior assaults, rapes, and attacks on female students. Id., at 729.

2. School's duty to protect resident students

In Verity v. State College (Mass. 1985) 539 N.E.2d 431, a student sued a college for negligence after being accosted while sleeping in her dorm room at 4:00 a.m., taken to the college dining hall, and raped. The plaintiff prevailed in the trial court, and the state supreme court affirmed. With regard to the existence of a duty, the court noted the existence of landlord-tenant cases (id., at 337 fn. 12) but for some reason did not base the college's duty on that relationship. Rather, it held that the college's duty was grounded on two other principles: (1) that as a matter of "existing social values and customs" colleges ordinarily exercise care to protect resident students, and (2) that one who voluntarily assumes a duty must perform with due care. Id., at 435-436.

With regard to foreseeability, the college's vice-president for operations, an individual defendant who established the security guards' patrol pattern and the campus lock system, admitted that he had foreseen the possibility that a student might be assaulted on campus. Also, the director of student affairs testified that she warned students at freshman orientation about the dangers of living at a women's college near a (cont'd)

Glossary

Acquittal: Legal judgment by either a jury or a judge that the accused is not guilty of the crime for which she was tried.

Action: Another word for lawsuit, case or litigation.

Adjournment: Postponing or rescheduling a court session until another date or time.

Adjudication: A final judicial determination of a case.

Affidavit: A written statement of facts sworn to under oath before a notary or public officer with authority to administer oaths. Affidavits are often used as supporting evidence for a motion.

Affirm: In appellate practice, to uphold a lower court's decision as valid.

Allegation: A statement or claim that has not yet been proved to be true or false.

Alternative dispute resolution (ADR): Methods of resolving disputes without official court proceedings, including mediation and arbitration.

Answer: A formal, written response to allegations made in a complaint or petition, in which the defendant admits or denies the allegations and sets out the grounds for his defense.

Appeal: A request for a higher court to review the legal rulings of a trial court or lower appellate court. The party who appeals is called the appellant and the one who responds to the appeal is the appellee or respondent.

Appellate court: A court that reviews lower court decisions.

Arbitration: A form of alternative dispute resolution in which parties submit their dispute to an impartial third person or persons. The arbitrators' decision, generally binding on both parties, follows an informal proceeding where each side presents evidence and witnesses.

Arraignment: A criminal defendant's first appearance in court, when she is informed of the charges against her and asked to plead guilty or not guilty.

Bail: Money or other property given by a criminal defendant as security for her appearance in court at a later date. If she fails to appear, the bail is forfeited.

Bench trial: Trial held before a judge without a jury. Unlike a jury trial, the judge decides both questions of facts as well as issues of law.

Bluebook: The Uniform System of Citation, which outlines the format for legal citation in all articles, briefs and papers.

Brief: A party's formal, written argument, usually submitted to support a motion or appeal, outlining legal reasons why the court should decide a particular issue in that party's favor.

Burden of proof: The obligation of a party to prove his allegations at trial and the standard of evidence required to convince a judge or jury. In a criminal action, the prosecution must prove the defendant guilty beyond a reasonable doubt. In a civil action, the plaintiff must usually establish that the defendant is liable by a preponderance of evidence or by clear and convincing evidence.

Capital offense: A crime punishable by death.

Caption: The heading that appears on all court papers in a proceeding, including the names of the parties to the lawsuit, the name of the court, the case number assigned and the title of the document (for example, complaint, motion to dismiss, reply).

Case law: The body of written decisions issued by the courts and published in case reporters.

Cause of action: Allegations that make up the grounds for a claim in a lawsuit. A complaint might contain several different causes of action.

Chambers: A judge's office.

Charge: In criminal law, a formal accusation by the prosecutor's office against a defendant.

Citation: Reference to a case, constitution, statute or legal treatise. A proper citation contains the name of the case or other authority, the book in which it is found, the volume in which it appears, its page or section number and the year it was decided or enacted.

Common law: The legal system that originated in England and is now used in the United States. Common law relies on the legal principles developed over time in judicial decisions (as opposed to statutory law, which is enacted by legislatures).

Complaint: A written statement filed in court to initiate a civil lawsuit. In it, the plaintiff identifies the defendant, the basis for the plaintiff's claim and the relief requested from the court. Sometimes this document is called a petition or pleading.

Contract: An enforceable promise or agreement between two or more persons.

Conviction: A judgment of guilt against a criminal defendant.

Counsel: Legal advice; a term also used to refer to lawyers in a case.

Court: Government entity with the authority to hear and resolve legal disputes.

Damages: Money paid by a defendant to a successful plaintiff in a civil case to compensate the plaintiff for her losses or injuries. Compensatory damages are awarded to cover the actual cost of an injury or loss. Punitive damages may be awarded to punish the defendant for willful or malicious acts.

Decision: A court's judgment or decree settling a dispute.

Default judgment: In a civil case, a judgment rendered in favor of the plaintiff because of the defendant's failure to answer or appear in court to contest the plaintiff's claim.

Defendant: In a civil suit, the person against whom a plaintiff brings suit; in a criminal case, the person formally accused of a crime.

Deposition: Sworn testimony taken outside court in the presence of attorneys for both sides. Depositions are often taken to examine potential witnesses or as part of discovery and can be used to impeach (discredit) a witness who later changes his story in court or when a witness is unavailable to testify at trial.

Discovery: The process of examination of documents and witnesses pertaining to the case to help lawyers prepare for trial. Each side can ask for and is obliged to turn over requested relevant documents. Typical discovery devices include depositions, interrogatories, requests for admissions and subpoenas.

Dismissal: A decision by a court to end a case for legal or other reasons.

Disposition: The final decision by the court in a dispute.

Due process: The standards for fair treatment of citizens by federal, state and local governments, including the courts.

equitable relief: A non-monetary award by a court when fairness suggests that money damages would be insufficient. Examples of equitable remedies include injunctions and temporary restraining orders.

Evidence: Information, including testimony, documents or physical objects, presented at trial to persuade a jury (or judge) of a party's version of the case.

Felony: A crime carrying a penalty of more than one year in prison.

File: To place a paper in the official custody of a court for entry into the record of a case.

Grand jury: A group of citizens assembled to hear the prosecution's evidence and decide whether there is probable cause to believe an individual committed an offense. If the grand jury votes yes, it issues an indictment.

Hearing: A formal legal proceeding other than a trial before a judicial officer or administrative body.

Information: A formal accusation issued by a prosecuting attorney (without grand jury involvement) charging a person with a crime.

Injunction: A court order prohibiting (or compelling) the performance of a specific act by a party to a lawsuit. It is a form of equitable relief.

Interrogatories: Written questions delivered by one side in a lawsuit to an opposing side as part of pre-trial discovery in civil cases. The party that receives the interrogatories must answer them in writing under oath.

Judge: Government official with authority to decide lawsuits brought before courts.

Judgment: The official decision of a court finally determining the outcome of a lawsuit.

Jurisdiction: Legal authority of a court to hear and decide a case; also refers to the geographic area over which the court has authority.

Jurisprudence: The study of law and the structure of the legal system.

Jury: A group of citizens selected to hear the evidence in a trial, to decide the facts and to declare a verdict.

Juvenile: A person younger than the legal age of adulthood (usually 18 years old).

Liability: The main issue to be determined in a civil case; a lawsuit turns on whether a civil defendant is liable for the claims and injuries alleged by the plaintiff.

Litigation: A case, controversy or lawsuit. The participants (plaintiffs/defendants or petitioners/respondents) in lawsuits are called litigants.

Litigator: An attorney who practices in the field of litigation.

Mediation: An alternative method of dispute resolution, where a neutral person meets with the parties to help reach a settlement without the procedures of a formal trial. Mediation is a non-adversarial process in which the parties need not have legal representation and the mediator has no power to impose a solution.

Misdemeanor: A less serious crime than a felony, punishable by less than a year of confinement.

Mistrial: A trial that has been declared void due to a fundamental or prejudicial error in the proceedings. When a mistrial is declared, the trial must start again with the selection of a new jury.

Motion: An application or request by one party to a court to decide a legal matter. Motions are often made before trial to resolve procedural issues or legal issues where there is no disagreement on the facts.

Nolo contendere: Latin term meaning "I will not contest it." In criminal cases, a plea of "no contest" has the same effect as a guilty plea in terms of sentencing but may not be considered an admission of guilt for any other purpose.

Opinion: A judge's written explanation of a decision of the court or of a majority of judges (for appellate decisions). A dissenting opinion may be issued by a judge who disagrees with the majority, and a judge might write a concurring opinion when she agrees with the majority's decision but has different reasons for reaching the same result.

Order: A decision or directive of a court.

Ordinance: A law enacted by a municipal body to enforce, control or limit certain activities.

Overrule: In appellate practice, when a higher court decides that a lower court's decision was in error.

Party: One of the litigants in a lawsuit; a person who sues or defends or is joined in a lawsuit.

Plaintiff: The person who initiates a civil lawsuit by filing a complaint..

Plea: In a criminal case, the defendant's formal response in court in answer to the charges against her ("guilty," "not guilty" or "nolo contendere").

Pleadings: In a civil case, the written statements filed with the court describing a party's legal or factual assertions (for example, the complaint, answer and reply).

Precedent: Earlier court decisions which provide guidelines for cases with similar facts and legal issues.

Presentence report: A report filed by the probation department to assist the judge in deciding the sentence of a guilty defendant.

Presumption: A fact assumed to be true under the law. For example, a criminal defendant is presumed to be innocent until the prosecution proves him guilty beyond a reasonable doubt.

Pro bono: Legal services provided free of charge (from the Latin phrase meaning "for the good").

Pro se: The status of a person who represents himself in court without an attorney (from the Latin for "on one's own behalf").

Procedure: The rules for the conduct of a lawsuit. There are separate rules for procedure in civil proceedings, criminal proceedings, federal, state and appellate courts.

Prosecute: To charge someone with a crime. A prosecutor tries a criminal case on behalf of the state or federal government. Prosecutors are elected or appointed officials known in different states as district attorneys, state's attorneys, county attorneys or prosecuting attorneys. Federal prosecutors work for the Office of the U.S. Attorney.

Public defender: A state-appointed defense attorney who represents those who cannot afford to hire their own attorney.

Record: A written account of all the proceedings in a lawsuit, including all pleadings, evidence, exhibits and judgment submitted. A record on appeal would also include a transcript of the testimony in the case.

Remand: In appellate practice, to send a case back to a lower court for further proceedings.

Reverse: (or overturn): In appellate practice, to set aside the decision of a lower court because of an error of law. A reversal is often followed by a remand.

Rules of evidence: Laws that determine what evidence may be admitted into a trial or hearing and under what circumstances.

Ruling: A decision made by a judge during the course of litigation.

Sentence: The punishment ordered by a court for a defendant convicted of a crime.

Sentencing guidelines: A set of rules and principles established by the U.S. Sentencing Commission for trial judges to determine the sentence of a convicted defendant in a federal criminal case.

Service of process: The delivery of legal papers to the opposing party. Rules of procedure prescribe the acceptable methods of delivery and written proof of service must generally be filed with the court.

Settlement: A resolution of parties' differences without a full trial.

Statute: A law passed by a legislature.

Statute of limitations: A law that sets the time within which parties must take action to enforce their rights. These deadlines vary depending on the kind of dispute, the circumstances of the case and the jurisdiction in which the suit is filed. A lawsuit filed after the deadline will be dismissed.

Stipulation: An agreement between parties in a litigation.

Subpoena: A command to a witness to appear and give testimony at a specific time and place.

Subpoena duces tecum: A command to a witness to appear and produce documents at a specific time and place.

Summary judgment: A decision made on the basis of statements and evidence presented for the record without a trial. A court may grant summary judgment when there is no dispute as to the facts of the case and one party is entitled to judgment as a matter of law.

Summons: In civil cases, a notice to a defendant or respondent that a complaint or petition was filed against him.

Testimony: Evidence presented orally by witnesses during trials, before grand juries or during administrative proceedings.

Tort: A civil wrong or breach of a duty to another person. A party injured by a tort may be entitled to sue for the harm suffered.

Transcript: A written, word-for-word record of what was said at a trial, hearing or deposition.

Trial court: The court in which a lawsuit is filed and where all litigation up to and including the trial is held.

Trial: A formal legal proceeding to resolve the disputes presented by a lawsuit.

U.S. attorney: A lawyer appointed by the president in each federal judicial district to prosecute and defend cases for the federal government. The Office of the U.S. Attorney has a staff of assistant U.S. attorneys who appear as the government's attorneys in individual cases.

Uphold: In appellate practice, to let stand the decision of a lower court.

Verdict: The final decision of a trial jury (or judge in a bench trial).

Voir dire: In jury selection, the process of interviewing prospective jurors for a trial.

Warrant: A written court order authorizing official action by law enforcement officials, such as an arrest or search.

White-collar crime: Refers to a particular kind of crime that doesn't involve violence or force but usually money or business.

Witness: A person called upon by either side in a lawsuit to give testimony before the court or jury.

Writ: A formal, written command or order issued by the court, requiring the performance of a specific act.

About the Author

Neeraja Viswanathan

Neeraja Viswanathan, JD (Fordham), lives in New York and is a journalist and a former litigation associate at Fried, Frank, Harris, Shriver and Jacobson.

Psst...
Need a Change in Venue?

Use the Internet's most targeted

job search tools for law

professionals.

Vault Law Job Board

The most comprehensive and convenient job board for law professionals. Target your search by area of law, function, and experience level, and find the job openings that you want. No surfing required.

VaultMatch Resume Database

Vault takes match-making to the next level: post your resume and customize your search by area of law, experience and more. We'll match job listings with your interests and criteria and e-mail them directly to your inbox.

VAULT
> the most trusted name in career information™

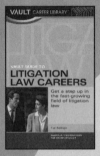

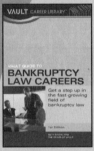

Psst...
Need a Change in Venue?

Use the Internet's most targeted
job search tools for law
professionals.

Vault Law Job Board

The most comprehensive and convenient job board for law
professionals. Target your search by area of law, function,
and experience level, and find the job openings that you want.
No surfing required.

VaultMatch Resume Database

Vault takes match-making to the next level: post your resume
and customize your search by area of law, experience and
more. We'll match job listings with your interests and criteria
and e-mail them directly to your inbox.